Trust Instead of Dominance

Marlitt Wendt

Trust
Instead of Dominance

Working towards a new form
of ethical horsemanship

Copyright © 2011 by Cadmos Publishing Ltd,
Richmond Upon Thames, UK
Copyright of original edition © 2010 Cadmos Verlag GmbH,
Schwarzenbek, Germany
Translation: Claire Williams
Design: Ravenstein + Partner, Verden
Setting: Das Agenturhaus, Munich
Cover photograph: Christiane Slawik
Content photos: Christiane Slawik
Editorial of original edition: Anneke Bosse
Editorial of this edition: Sarah Binns
Printed by: Westermann Druck, Zwickau

British Library Cataloguing in Publication Data
A catalogue record of this book is available from the
British Library.

Printed in Germany

ISBN 978-0-85788-001-7

CONTENTS

Trust instead of Dominance

CONTENTS
Trust instead of Dominance

So tell me, riders, how do you feel about domination?

In recent years dominance seems to have become one of the key focuses of discussion and debate. Terms such as domination, control, dominance problems, hierarchy and dominance training seem to be on the lips of so many riders and trainers. Entire training methods rely on these terms and the models used to explain them. But do we really always have to dominate our horses? Are dominance and hierarchy really as significant in a horse's day to day life as we are led to believe? And in many cases doesn't a training system based on dominance do more harm than good?

Much of the terminology used by dominance-based trainers when explaining their systems comes originally from equine behavioural science. In spite of the advances within this branch of science some of the earlier ideas have been integrated into training methods, often without a full understanding of them. The typical behaviour of a herd, which has its own social structure and hierarchy, isn't as obvious and one-dimensional as has been taught for decades. Meanwhile the scientific world is also seriously questioning the existence of a purely dominance-based hierarchy, both within a herd and in relation to humans. The stallions and mares of legend that take over leadership of their herds, and about whom much has been written, exist only in fairy tales. In addition, the question has to be asked whether training methods that rely for their basis on the principles of so-called 'Dominance-based training' really work in the way you are led to believe, or whether in fact the learning process behind them has nothing at all to do with establishing a new pecking order. The alleged absence of force in so many of these methods has to be strongly questioned.

Life as experienced in a herd, and the relationships that horses have with each other and with the people around them, leave a mark on other natural laws of behaviour. In this book I would like to try to dispel some of this confusion and give you an insight into a horse's social life from a behavioural science perspective. In addition I will analyse horses' natural associations and the tangle of their herd relationships as well as observing their relationship to humankind and our training methods. In doing this we will be able to paint a new picture of a horse's social life and investigate an alternative method of training, which involves a more ethical type of interaction between horse and human.

This book should help you to assess different types of training methods for their understanding of equine behaviour and their freedom from force. I also hope to be able to give my readers the ability to differentiate between positive and negative training methods – whether at shows, competitions, or when choosing a trainer for your own horse. In being able to do this we are also contributing towards a more peaceful coexistence between humankind and the horse.

Marlitt Wendt, August 2010

Horses – more than a herd animal

An introduction to the world of the horse

All horses are not the same. Although any casual observer can see clear and marked differences between individual representatives of the species with the melodic sounding scientific name *Equus ferus caballus*, most books on horses and riders speak with one voice about 'the horse'. However, there is as much a typical horse as there is a typical human. There are clear differences to be found, both behaviourally and physically, between Arabs and Exmoor ponies, Belgian Draught horses and Mongolian horses, or between Hanoverians and Quarter Horses. In addition, representatives from within individual breeds can also differ greatly in their behaviour and characteristics. It is precisely this individuality that characterises horses and which provides so many of the challenges that we find when dealing with them. No one horse is exactly like any other, so we are faced continuously with new surprises when involved with them. In what follows, I will cover where our leisure partners of today come from and highlight some of their evolutionary qualities, so that we are prepared for our later discussion of some of their characteristic features.

Where does the horse come from and where is it going?

In the course of the millions of years that form its developmental history, the horse has learned to adapt to different living conditions and circumstances. In the course of its evolution, and as a result of certain inherited traits being passed down from generation to generation, the species we now know as the horse underwent significant anatomical and physical changes. What started as an antelope-like forest-dwelling animal became a plains-living animal that could gallop – the horse. Distinguishing characteristics of an individual are coded in the form of genes, which are copied and passed on to the following generations. Many species don't exist in just a single form, but have a number of different variations. The hereditary differences among individuals, in other words the genetic variability, are created by these different forms and the recombination or reordering of their genes.

Even in the case of the ancestors of our domesticated horses, there has always been a wide variety of subspecies or types that have adapted to the climatic and ecological conditions of different regions around the world. Today, in order to trace the ancestry

Today's breeds are a colourful mix, originating from very different types. They unite a wide range of behavioural characteristics inherited from their ancestors.

of horses and their domestication, researchers make use of the genetic information contained within the so-called mitochondrial DNA (mtDNA), which is passed on exclusively from mother to daughter. Normally the order of the genes changes in every generation owing to the merging of the female and male elements at conception; however, when considering mtDNA, you are dealing with a recognisable component of the genes that remains consistent over many generations, and through which it is possible to follow the maternal line and the degree of relationship between different species of equines. The origins of the maternal line of the modern domesticated horse, and thus the ancestress of all of the various different types of horse, can be traced back between 320,000 and 630,000 years. Using mitochondrial DNA, the domestication of the horse by humankind can be traced back to the period between 9400 and 2000 BC.

For a long period, researchers hypothesised that the horse of today originated from a single ancestor, a theory that is now strongly doubted. They imagined that the domestication of the horse was a single and relatively simple process, which caused the domesticated horse we ride today to be created from the interbreeding and natural selection of only a few individuals, which were then spread around the world by humankind. Modern research now assumes that the domestication of the horse took place in a number of different locations around the world, and at varying times. Each group of people took the horses that were living in their region at that time and in effect created their own 'ancestral' horse through breeding. This theory is supported by the fact that, when examining the current range of horses that exist today, we can find 17 different types with varying maternal lines.

The origins of today's breeds

The different subspecies mentioned above are the ancestors of today's domesticated horses and thus the foundation for the modern breeds of today. Their initial development occurred without the influence of humankind, and was a result only of exposure to the environment in which they lived in different parts of the world. They therefore developed great differences not only in their physical characteristics but also in their behaviour. Probably the oldest domesticated type of horse, with a maternal line that stretches back 47,000 to 166,000 years, originated on the steppes of Asia and was characterised by a short-backed, slight body, a short head with wide nostrils and a tendency to move fast in its dry, warm habitat. These horses formed very close family groups and found it easier than the other types of horses to become used to humans.

The maternal lines of the northern draught breeds (sometimes inaccurately referred to as cold-blooded horses) can be traced back 29,000 to 100,000 years. With their thickset and chunky bodies and powerful jaws adapted to chewing hardier grasses, they were perfectly suited to cold climates. This was a horse that went everywhere at a steady walk and formed loose groups.

The maternal line of the more roman-nosed warmblood type, which is 6000 to 21,000 years old, was well suited to the vast, cold steppes of the northern hemisphere. They had a relatively long back and long limbs that were ideally suited for long journeys. They probably lived a solitary life, with herd life virtually unknown, with the exception of groups of older mares who lived with other female family members. It can be assumed from this that these horses would have tended towards showing more aggressive behaviour and would have had a well developed sense of personal space.

The particular way in which various breeds express themselves can easily lead to misunderstandings when strange horses meet for the first time.

The social life of the maternal line of the first ponies, 2000 to 8000 years old, probably took place in large herds, which fell into individual subgroups but joined together when danger threatened. With their medium size and their thick coats they were especially well suited to the mild, damp climate of the British Isles and Scandinavia.

In addition to these four basic types, there were other varieties of early horse from which our ancestors developed what would become today's breeds. But, as can be seen, the beginnings of our domestic horses were, in terms of their social behaviour and environment, very different. There were horses that developed in very close family groups and others that lived a rather more solitary existence. As a result of this, the reality is that it is illogical to assume that there is a single and uniform herd and hierarchical structure that applies to the full range of horses that exist today. From domesticated horses with a variety of origins, humankind has bred and developed the current breeds over many centuries. Some of today's breeds are still very close in type to their ancestors, others are a result of crossing several types, uniting some of their characteristics, both physical and behavioural.

Local dialects in the equine kingdom

The range of expressions covers a wide spectrum among the different breeds of horse. As a result of this, individuals from different breeds can sometimes find it hard to understand each other. What for one might be a friendly tussle could for another be a serious fight.

The way certain elements of behaviour, body language and facial expressions are shown or expressed can also vary considerably. Whilst an Arabian horse will hold his tail upright at the slightest excitement in a way that is typical for this breed, this type of behaviour is likely to be seen much more rarely in a Belgian heavy horse, and then only in cases of extreme provocation.

We can also clearly distinguish differences in threatening behaviour. Owing to its smaller muzzle, a Welsh pony's more oval nostrils appear a lot less threatening than the nostrils of a French trotter, even when pulled into a much narrower slit, although both individuals may be making a threat with the same intensity. Many thoroughbred types tend towards a pattern of behaviour that is more extravagant, while heavy horses use only a minimal number of physical changes to show their mental state.

These differences in the way horses express themselves are probably founded in the variety of subspecies from which horses originated. While thoroughbreds originally would have had to communicate with each other over larger distances, ponies, living as they did in closer proximity to each other, could rely on smaller gestures because their body language did not have to be read at great distances. Owing to the mixing of these different types over time in our modern breeds, many of the behavioural patterns from different types can be found within the same breed. This means that there is a much wider breadth of behavioural characteristics than would have been the case originally. Different types of horses don't naturally know the habits and language of others, but instead have to learn them. The individual pattern of behaviour that they have learned in their own herd has been taught to them by their parents, siblings and other members of the herd. If the equine family, as is the case in most breeding establishments, consists of representatives of only one breed, a foal will not learn how to assess the often different social behaviour of other breeds. In some cases these 'cultural' differences in understanding can be so great that it may be better for horses to remain separated so that both sides can live in peace. It is therefore sensible to allow foals to get accustomed to different breeds and types so that they can cope more easily when they encounter them in later life.

Many ponies, many personalities.

The horse as an individual

Besides the differences in behaviour among the various types of horse, there are also well developed unique characteristic qualities that appear within individual breeds. Sometimes these differences among representatives of the same breed can be even greater than those among different breeds. Owing to its genetic make-up and it own experiences, each horse is a unique individual with a distinctive character and its own special personality. Accordingly, some characteristics may be developed to a greater or lesser degree in some horses compared with others.

We all have an idea about what shapes our personality or our character. We understand that this includes our moods, as well as all those frequently repeated individual behavioural patterns that become remembered as our characteristics. Just as we can recognise

tell what mood they are in by their body language. We give our horses names and recognise their personalities. A true understanding of the differences among them assumes, however, a certain background knowledge and empathy. We need to take an introverted horse and its characteristics just as seriously as those of an extrovert and consider all the differing types of personality that exist.

Animal of flight, of the steppes and of the herd: an incomplete model

Using the labels 'herd', 'steppe' or 'flight' to describe the horse does it an injustice. As we have already seen, thanks to the variety of origins that our horses are derived from and the resultant breeds that emerged, there are wide differences in their social and stress behaviour and how they express this. Herd behaviour exists; however not every horse at every stage of its life is a herd animal. A horse may display flight behaviour, but a horse can just as appropriately be described as an 'animal of flight' as a person can be called a 'family man', to the exclusion of all else.

A typical herd of ponies will form a much tighter group than a herd of warmbloods. Both are herds, but with different rules and habits. Both groups are, in their own way, typical of horses and have to be viewed equally, side by side.

Similarly, just because of its genetic origins you can't label every horse as an animal of the steppes. The ancestor of our ponies, for example, didn't have long enough legs for crossing the steppes of Asia. It was much more suited to the environment featuring woods and plenty of rain, from which it originated. Very different types of horses also

someone by their physical appearance, we also have a picture or idea of their typical behaviour and moods, in other words the characteristics that make them the individual they are. One person can have a cheerful nature; another may be more of a lone wolf. In the case of yet another person we may appreciate that their character is more complex and can't be labelled so easily. The same is true for our horses: we observe typical patterns of behaviour again and again, and can, for example,

Not every horse is necessarily a typical animal of flight.

emerged on the steppes, because of the different natural conditions seen in the ecosystems that made up either the 'arid steppes' – very dry and hot areas – or the 'Tundra steppes' – the vast cold northern plains.

This means that you can't describe a 'typical' horse as a herd animal, just as you can't give one definition or draw one picture of what a 'steppe' horse looks like. As a result of their distinctive origins, the way different horses live, what they eat and their behavioural characteristics will all vary greatly.

Flight is not automatically the only behaviour that a horse might show as a reaction to fear. There are horses that freeze at the first sign of danger and others that react by attacking the source of danger. To label a heavy horse, typical of its breed, as the classical animal of flight when faced with danger doesn't live up to the reality.

A simplified model of behaviour described by the concept of the horse as one of three types –herd, steppes or flight – is nowhere near being a close representation of reality. This model cannot begin to detail all the different facets of equine behaviour, and so remains a gross over-simplification. Unfortunately though, simplified models all

While a thoroughbred is usually easily excitable, a typical draught horse tends to freeze at a sign of danger.

too often become the new 'truth' and develop into the basis for ground-breaking new theories in horse training. Be very cautious when this happens. If the basic assumptions of certain training methods rely on outdated scientific theories, then the views formed of a horse's nature arising from them should not be relied upon. Many horse trainers, for example, talk of recreating a horse's 'natural flight instinct', in other words making the horse run away, by using a whip to drive the horse away. When they do this, however, they are overlooking the fact that not every type of horse follows this pattern of behaviour and may, instead of running away, react to their fear by freezing on the spot. A trainer is not doing justice to the complex nature of an individual horse by the simple equation of 'chasing = flight'.

One horse is not the same as another

If you were to open the pages of a horse magazine and read any of the popular articles about horses, you would quickly notice that they always deal with the stereotypical horse. The horse always lives in a herd, the horse is an animal of flight, the horse lives in a structure similar to a harem, the horse is mature by the age of seven and so on. At best it might be mentioned that there is of course a great deal of variation, but there is not enough emphasis on the marked differences.

Why then is only one type of horse described? Simplification is almost inevitable, because we humans need it in order to get to grips with our increasingly complex world. In addition, it is of course sensible to view our horses' behaviour in a simplified way initially, so that we can add increasingly complicated facts to our understanding of their behaviour.

Sometimes, though, simplification can be dangerous, for example when we can't do justice to a horse's true nature or, at worst, when clever trainers make straightforward assumptions from this over-simplification and want to make a name for themselves at the horse's expense.

When someone wants to make robust and accurate statements about a horse's nature and behaviour they have to be very careful with their observations. They should always collect their data objectively, and the data should be able to be verified statistically. This issue is at the root of the debate around

Allow every horse to be an individual – this is the human's most important role.

'equine studies'. Most of the data stemming from so-called horse gurus originate from their own personal, and thus subjective, experiences. Many of these observations do not bear up to scientific scrutiny and can really only be seen as anecdotal rather than scientific in nature. Of course, many a Californian horse trainer has had a lot of practical experience with horses in their life. However, it is unlikely that they will have saved their data in any scientifically recognisable form.

It is also important to understand that a statistical value can never predict the future behaviour of an individual animal. A study will always produce certain generalised descriptive characteristics. A researcher wants to reach conclusions about a species in an evolutionary context and not in terms of the individual grazing in its field. In science, theories, not truths, are developed; in other words explanatory models are developed and these last for as long as it takes for a better explanation to be found. Many horse trainers pick out certain aspects or use terminology from the field of behavioural science and construct their own training methods targeted at whatever is currently 'in'. In contrast to the scientific world, however, these methods then become 'truths' written in stone that are purported to be able to predict our horses' future behaviour.

A patchwork family

The classical herd structure and its variations

A horse in the wild usually will live as part of a herd, because a herd offers certain advantages. Many eyes see better than two, so together they can defend themselves against enemies. A herd member can fall back on the experiences of other herd members when faced with different situations. A herd is a collection of animals that know one another, form a collective group and to the outside world form a unit that can act as one. But here we come to the first hitch: not every collection of horses is necessarily a herd! Large groups of horses put out together will often divide up into various subgroups that coexist in the same field but will only join up together at signs of danger. A herd is identified by the existence of a social group structure and the fact that the members of the group know each other individually. Since horses can't personally learn to know an unlimited number of other horses, a large group of more than 20 animals will always form into subgroups. In this chapter I would like to introduce the findings from current behavioural science research studies and explain their significance to the way we group together horses in our care.

Some stallions form deep friendships with other stallions that last a lifetime.

Different ways of living together

In the natural world there is a confusing variety of possible combinations of groupings and ways of cooperating within species, and even more so in the case of horses in the care of humans. Let's begin with the simplest type – a single horse. Unfortunately many domesticated horses are forced into an isolated existence which never occurs in nature – or does it? On the contrary, even in nature these loners do occur at times. As a rule they are usually young mares that have been driven out of the herd but who usually quickly find another stallion's herd to join, young stallions that are searching for a group of similar bachelors to join, or sometimes fully grown but older stallions. However, this lone existence is rare in the wild and is very much the exception. In any case, in the natural world, a loner has chosen this existence of their own free will and so can't be compared to the many stallions who have an isolated existence forced upon them by the way they are stabled. This isolation, in which horses are kept without contact with others, is neither fair nor appropriate for the species and is quite rightly banned under legislation that prevents cruelty to animals in countries such as Germany and the UK.

If we look at a horse that is able to organise its own life in a natural or wild state, then the smallest possible 'herd' consists of two individuals. Some horses form such a deep relationship with their partner that they spend a long time with each other and seem to be able to live without any other company. Furthermore some stallions have such a pronounced preference for a particular mare that gradually the other mares in their harems will migrate to other herds. Often this pairing will produce offspring that remain as part of a 'mini herd' for a while, but adult members will not join up with it. Mostly though, this pairing is the start of a new and larger family. A young inexperienced stallion joins up with a mare, and is gradually joined by other mares and their offspring.

Stallions too sometimes live together in pairs. This can either be the start of what will later be described as a bachelor group, or this pairing might be based on two males bonding to form a deep friendship or a close family relationship, such as occurs between brothers. Sometimes adult stallions will still roam around in pairs after they have lived together in a larger group of bachelors. They will help each other out and may even later look to join another group together. Such a friendship can even go so far that they may later share a harem of mares.

If a stallion should die, his mares are left on their own. Once they come into season the mares will quickly find another stallion or will be encouraged forcibly by a stallion to join his harem. Outside of the breeding season, though, mares are often very choosy when it comes to selecting a new stallion. They will make their own choice and in general won't be forced into joining a particular herd. For this reason it is possible for herds to exist that consist only of mares with no male companion.

And now we come finally to what some people think of as the true 'normal' herd structure, and to which many trainers refer: the so-called family unit that consists of a mature stallion and differing numbers of mature mares and their offspring living together. Here we are dealing with a common structure that remains stable over many years. Earlier it was thought that the stallion led his group unchallenged and could be designated as the highest ranking alpha animal, hence the

The family group within herds of wild horses is one
of many different forms of coexistence.

term 'dominant' or 'lead stallion'. Later it was
realised that individual mares played just
as important a role as the stallion, hence the
term 'lead mare' and the idea of a division
of labour amongst the sexes. We will see
later what an over-simplification this represents.

I am me

Every horse has its own personal space,
a zone around its body that others can
only enter into when permitted – and
even then this is usually restricted to
horses that are either already known or

A horse has its own personal space and may react to an unwanted intrusion from another horse by stamping its foot.

related. This personal space can vary greatly in size. In the case of some breeds and individuals it can be very small. Thus a number of Shetland ponies might stand clustered around a hayrack with their bodies touching, while a group of thoroughbred mares might need five metres space around each of them in order to be able to eat without feeling cramped. There can be pronounced differences in the scale of each individual's personal space and how strongly it is felt, and the effect of this will carry over into real-life situations. Within a horse's individual space the rules of hierarchy also lose their force. It is an area about which they make their own decisions and is taboo to everyone else. Humans also have greatly differing sensitivities when it comes to personal space. While in some cultures it is common to embrace each other effusively or kiss cheeks when meeting, in others it is enough to politely shake the other's hand. Personal space is thus dependent on the individual's inherent personality, on how they have been socialised, and on the prevailing culture.

Pairs – the strongest link in an equine family

Alongside family groupings, of particular significance within equine society are pair-bonds or pair relationships. Two horses may form a deep and firm friendship, often lasting many years. These friendships can even survive membership of different family groups. The horses will feed together and each will form the most important social partner for the other. If such a bond exists between a stallion and one of his mares, the stallion will spend more time with this mare and will cover her more frequently

A bachelor group is a loose association of members that change frequently. Under the protection of the group, young stallions can mature to become well balanced individuals.

Boys alone – bachelor groups

Given that there are about the same number of stallions born as mares, in addition to the family groups with one stallion at the head, there must also be groups of males – otherwise many stallions would have to live by themselves. Living together in groups always holds considerable advantages for horses, so young stallions will often form groups of their own. These bachelor groups can last for many years, although the members of the group will change more frequently than is the case with family groups. One stallion may leave because he has joined up with a mare to start a family, while another may be driven away from the family group by his father and will join the bachelor group and grow to maturity under the protection of the others. These herds of young bachelor stallions will have a very loose social structure with fluctuating membership.

Stallions united

Pair-bonded stallions may share mares, living more or less side by side with equal rights. Such cooperation can be very worthwhile. Although each stallion in this grouping will potentially only sire half of the foals born, each will also have a strong partner at his side to help him with the defence and security of the group. Each of the stallions therefore has more time during the day to rest and is likely to stay fit and healthy for longer. Such stallions may also remain with a group of mares over a longer period and thus sire

than the others. Pairs will spend much time with each other during the day, often grazing close together, standing nose to tail to offer protection to the other from flies, walking around together and carrying out intensive sessions of mutual grooming.

United we're strong!

more offspring throughout their lifetime. In a biological sense this is especially sensible in the case of related stallions. Two brothers are still closely related to the offspring of the other, so this can prove to be a very successful strategy from an evolutionary perspective. In evolution it is all about passing on hereditary characteristics from one generation to the next. Animals that are related can therefore pass on the genetic material to the next generation not only through their own offspring but also through the offspring of their relatives.

There will also be mature male offspring that remain inconspicuous, never having made any approaches towards the mares. Males such as this will be tolerated by the dominant stallion as being a subordinate companion. Stallions such as this are likely to be kept at a distance when the mares come into season, but will live alongside them for the rest of the year.

Step by step into adulthood

Young stallions are usually sexually mature by the time they are one year old; however, depending on the type of horse and its individual development some may be mature by eight months and others only at two years old. At this stage they will become more independent and distance themselves gradually from the family they were born into. Either they will be driven away by the dominant stallion when showing too strong an interest in the mares within the family group, or they will of their own accord seek out a bachelor group nearby or a solo mare. Young mares tend to stay with the group they were born into for much longer, sometimes for their entire life. When they reach sexual maturity at about the age of two years they will either be 'kidnapped' by a stallion from outside the family group, or they may leave the group independently, which naturally gets around the problem of inbreeding.

A journey into the world of behavioural science

It is only possible to observe and interpret the behaviour of animals if you examine not only the theory of evolution, as mentioned in the first chapter, but also further biological facts about the behaviour of living things.

The game of life

Game Theory is a theory of evolutionary science that predicts that when no one single behavioural strategy is always a winner, a number of different strategies may exist in the population, which are used by different individuals. Everyone plays according to their strengths and, as long as you are successful sooner or later, your genes will survive. It is assumed that a certain type of strategic behaviour is stable, in evolutionary terms,

Horses within a herd often go around together as couples. They enjoy a close relationship and go through life side by side.

meaning that it is consistently shown in horses over many generations. If there isn't just a single strategy that, when one is faced with a specific problem, is guaranteed to result in reaching the goal (in other words a win), but rather a number of possibilities, then these various possibilities will continue to live on as evolutionarily stable options within a population. Every horse plays this game for its own life or death as well as its physical and mental qualities allow. If it is successful, it passes on its strategy as one of the options to its offspring.

To explain this phenomenon further, we just need to imagine a typical problem for a typical

The behaviour of the same horse can range between rough and gentle. Horses adapt their conduct according to their particular companions and the current situation.

stallion. The stallion's instinct is to want to father as many foals as possible, so he requires a strategy that helps him fulfil this aim. The best known strategy is to live as a stallion with his own harem. The advantage of this is that the stallion could sire a large number of offspring, but the cost of this is that he lives with the threat of danger and under a great deal of pressure due to the heightened need for energy, the continual stress of reproduction and defending his mares, as well as the constant risk of injury through having to fight off other stallions. For a strong, powerful fully grown stallion this might be the best strategy; however it wouldn't be sensible for nature to allow only a limited number of stallions to reproduce. The genetic variation in horses, which allows the species to adapt itself to a variety of changing environmental situations, would be diluted after only a few generations.

There also needs to be a way for other, less strong or younger, stallions to play the game of life. There has to be a mechanism that ensures more evenness and balance. For this reason many stallions attach themselves to bachelor groups that remain close to herds and wait for a moment that gives them the chance to mate with a mare.

This strategy can be successful for many stallions, not just when young but for their entire life. A stallion living like this avoids all of the work and responsibilities that life as a stallion with a harem brings, and despite this enjoys the protection of a group while also managing to sire offspring. This phenomenon has been proven by studies showing that the dominant stallion is not always the biological father of all the foals in his herd, but only a certain percentage of them. A considerable proportion of the foals will have been sired when mares were 'unfaithful' with

stallions from a nearby group of bachelors. Mares appreciate the presence of the strong dominant stallion as a protector for their foals, but might not always chose him as the father of their offspring.

An additional successful strategy can be for a young stallion to live as long as possible inconspicuously under the protection of the harem stallion, without challenging him and only at his death stepping into his shoes.

Game Theory can be applied in many spheres of life. There will undoubtedly be a large number of individuals that stick by the established rules of the game, but there are specific percentages that play the game according to their own rules. For this reason, in nature there is a great range of possible behaviours and traits among horses.

Kin selection

The term 'kin selection', also known as 'relative selection', reflects a basic principle in the nature of family relationships. To secure the continuation of the horse as a species and the passing on of its own genetic material, a horse needs to produce as many offspring as possible. Given, however, that a filly foal will always have at least 50 per cent of the genetic material of each of her siblings, it makes sense to ensure their survival. We can see this apparently unselfish behaviour of mares in the way in which they devotedly look after the offspring produced by their own mother. In reality they are selfishly securing their own genetic material, and natural selection will be influenced towards the direction of their own relatives.

This leads us to ask the question whether horses act selfishly, in other words egoistically, or whether they act altruistically, for the sake of the wider community. The fundamental theory, that every living being is fighting to spread its own genes, would suggest that every animal should behave strictly egoistically. In some cases, as described in the example given of kin selection, in an evolutionary sense it is more sensible to act for the benefit of others rather than for oneself. This also occurs in the case of reciprocal altruism. This involves animals mutually helping each other out, and it works as long as opportunities arise often enough to repay the debt to the other. It is an example of treating others as you wish to be treated by them. Nature gives horses the opportunity to help each other, and then they return the favour. This principle is particularly obvious when it comes to horses scratching each other on the withers. One horse scratches the other, on the one hand to make it itself feel better and cement the relationship, and on the other hand to have the favour reciprocated. Thus both get something out of the behaviour.

The optimal skew theory says that the optimal division of the reproduction in a population is dependent as much on the environment as on the degree of relationship of the horses. The example of our adolescent, inconspicuous stallion shows this. If in the immediate vicinity there are few enemies and many unattached mares, then it would make most biological sense to find his own harem quickly and produce offspring. If however there is no availability of mares and the habitat is barren and limited in size, then the better alternative may be to wait for the opportunity to take the harem over and in the meantime protect the offspring of his mother and sisters.

The concept of gender

What makes a man a man and a woman a woman? Are the obvious differences really of a biological nature or more of a social or psychological nature? In the case of horses, the question must also be asked whether specific behavioural patterns can be assigned to a specific gender or whether they can be attributed to the qualities of an individual under certain conditions. Some patterns of behaviour will be shown, depending on the context, by both stallions and mares. Up until now only a few generalisations could be made about the behaviour of one gender that didn't also, in individual cases, apply to the other. So we observe mares that cover another horse's droppings with their own, just as a stallion would, or we may even see a mare that tries to mate with another. Similarly, there are stallions that spend a lot of time scratching and grooming their foals, which is usually the job of the mother. Gender appears to be a semantic concept, which leads us to compartmentalise certain types of behaviour into a specific 'gender drawer'.

Friendships exist not only within a herd but also between members of two different herds.

Contact with other horses and herds

Horses not only have contact with the members of their own group but they also cultivate friendships outside of this unit. Given that horses as a rule are not territorial and are happy to coexist with others, different groups will tend to live in more or less close contact. They will meet at a shared waterhole, or perhaps rest together in a dry or sheltered area, and then graze far apart during the day. Many groups get to know each other very well over the years. Foals from family A will play with those from family B, mares will mix together, and even mature stallions from different groups have been observed grooming each other – with no obvious sign of hostility. Of course such contact is less extensive during the mating season, but this only affects a relatively short part of the year.

Is blood thicker than water?

For horses, relatives are the glue that keeps their social order stuck together. Mares look after their foals devotedly and frequently maintain contact with their filly foals over their entire life. Siblings also remain close.

Older sisters learn from seeing how their younger siblings are raised and use this to effect when they become mothers themselves.

Do horses really show preferences for other members of the same breed or for those of the same coat colour? It is often claimed that horses will only get on really well with those

Foals learn what it is to be a foal through early socialisation.

of the same breed or with other horses that are the same colour. Experiments, however, have shown that no general pattern could be shown in preferences for certain breeds or colours.

A horse probably does not have a real idea of what it looks like, its coat colour, or its breed. Over the course of its youth there is a process called socialisation, during which a horse will unconsciously learn what is 'normal' and what is not. If, for example, it lives in a group that consists exclusively of Icelandic ponies, then later it is likely to feel drawn to this type of horse and will not accept other horses with different characteristics as easily.

The colour of its mother and siblings will also be imprinted on a foal. Given that coat colour is hereditary, it may well be that a foal lives with only bay horses and once fully grown may take longer to befriend a skewbald or a leopard-spotted Appaloosa. How pronounced this preference is will vary greatly from horse to horse. It can be so strong, however, that some stallions will not accept mares of a certain colour and not cover them when they are in season.

From day one a foal will watch its mother carefully. It will adopt many of her preferences and copy her behaviour.

Name and rank

Equine social structure

Herd life is marked by various social structures, friendships and relationships. The roles of both the stallions and mares will change substantially depending on the situation they are living in. The position within a specific group, such as a bachelor group or a family, the number of horses of the same sex, the presence of offspring and the hormonal cycle will all influence the social structure. Horses are masters of adaptability. While one horse may remain inconspicuous or behave submissively in a group of horses turned out together, the same horse in a different grouping can behave very differently and find itself in a different position within the group. In doing this the horse will adapt its body language to fit with the situation and who is standing opposite it. Body language is always dependent on the individual a horse is 'speaking' to. The horse will vary the signals according to whether they are communicating with a human, a strange stallion or a foal. This chapter gives an overview of the flexible social structure that applies to horses.

Very different from a pecking order, the hierarchy within herds is a complex system that can only be understood through detailed studies.

Complex hierarchical relationships

People have a natural tendency to look for sense and order within their own world and then to think that they recognise this everywhere else. Simple explanations give us the apparent security of being able to understand our environment, but unfortunately nature turns out to be considerably more complex once you look closer and start to analyse it.

One of these simplified human models is the principle of a fixed hierarchy within a herd. In the equestrian world this idea has been in existence for a long time, because it promises people the apparent security of taking up a position of leadership over the horse and thus being able to predict and control its behaviour in the future. We are probably all aware of common terms used in relationship to hierarchy, such as alpha animal, dominant behaviour, and rank, all of which come from the field of behavioural science. In the following sections I would like to provide an overview of the meaning of the central concepts of herd behaviour in horses from a behavioural science perspective.

Definition of hierarchy

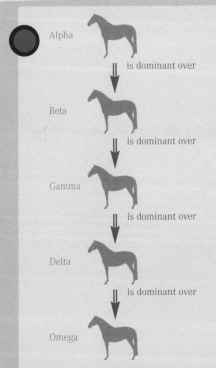

Alpha

is dominant over

Beta

is dominant over

Gamma

is dominant over

Delta

is dominant over

Omega

Graphic 1:
The hierarchy within a herd was once thought to be like a ladder, in which the alpha animal at the top of the hierarchy dominated all those below them and the omega animal was at the bottom, subjugated by all the others. New insights show that the relationships within a herd are not structured as simply as this.

Linear vs network relationships

In modern behavioural science, many researchers have tried for a long time to get the theory of a linear hierarchy to stick. But up until now equine behavioural researchers have only been able to detail triangular relationships or more complicated forms than a straight line hierarchy. You can picture this as an example in which A is dominant over B, B is dominant over C, while C is dominant over A. Who is higher ranking? The answer is irrelevant, because a hierarchy doesn't represent an order like the rungs on a ladder, but represents more of a spider's web or network of relationships, which include individual personality traits. Even in groups where a hierarchy can be seen to exist at a certain point in time, at a later time it may not be seen any longer. There is no evidence that a horse can have a permanent dominant position over another for its entire life.

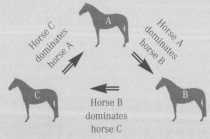

Horse C dominates horse A

Horse A dominates horse B

A

C

Horse B dominates horse C

B

Graphic 2:
Horses do not form linear hierarchies, but rather more complex shapes such as triangular relationships, in which no one dominant horse can be recognised.

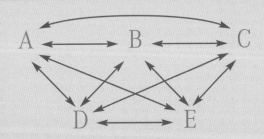

A ⟷ B ⟷ C
D ⟷ E

Graphic 3:
Every horse cultivates contacts with other members of its herd. The more horses that are involved and the more different areas of life are covered, the more complicated is the network of relationships.

Arguments between horses are very obvious and therefore easy to observe. To establish where a horse stands in the hierarchy, behavioural researchers must pay close attention to the often very subtle signals being communicated.

Science understands hierarchy to be a system in which the status of a single animal in a group can be described or accounted for within a specific period and with the help of precisely defined recognisable behaviour. The individual rank refers to the assumed position. A horse that is higher in rank should enjoy more privileges than others, but should also have to fulfil more duties, such as leading the group. It is a mistake though to believe that the higher ranking animal generally gets all the benefits. Biologically it makes no sense to waste energy on something that you really don't need. No horse is going to defend a grazing area the size of a football field because it can't eat it all at once and would waste more energy constantly chasing other horses away than it could build up in the same amount of time. In the life of a horse, and thus also in the establishment of a hierarchy, the main concerns are access to essential resources such as feed, social contact or mates – all aimed at securing survival.

So that there is no need, for example, to fight for their feeding place at every feed time, horses establish a hierarchy that helps them to demonstrate their own status and recognise the positions of the other members of the herd. This should avoid conflict and strengthen the herd structure.

It is a complicated process to identify a horse's position in the hierarchy, and can't be, as is maintained by some trainers, established within a few minutes just by casually looking at the animals. Rather it requires hundreds of hours of data recording, which then have to be analysed using a variety of statistical methods, and the results of this costly process only lead to conclusions relating to the period that has been observed. It is not possible to produce predictions about future behaviours using these methods and they can't give exact conclusions about the structure of a group. These snapshots allow the biologist only an initial impression of the complex structure of the herd.

Once the scientist has established the herd ranking, then theoretically they could classify each individual horse within this structure. Following the Greek alphabet, the alpha animal would be at the top and be dominant over all those below. This would then be followed by the beta animal, which is dominant over all those except the alpha horse. All other members of the herd would then follow in a specific order until the omega animal, the lowest ranking horse in the herd, was reached. A hierarchy that is assigned in this way, on the basis of a specific characteristic such as the aggressiveness of each member of the group, allows the horses to be put into an order like rungs on a ladder and should only be seen as a very simplified model. The complex social structure that exists within a herd of horses is multi-layered and cannot be based on such a simple linear hierarchy, especially when the number of networks involved in equine social coexistence is considered.

In some animal societies, such as those of cats, alongside full members of the hierarchy there are also 'pariahs' that have no real bonds with the group and are in effect rejected and excluded, being totally ignored by the other group members. Occasionally this phenomenon can be seen with very old or weak horses.

Lead stallion and lead mare

In earlier publications the alpha animal was portrayed as a kind of absolute ruler that had sole authority over all facets of life. Depending on whether it was male or female, this animal was referred to as the lead stallion or lead mare. The use of the word 'lead' is based on the fact that the term refers to an especially experienced horse that is able to lead the herd members through all situations that they may face and be able to protect them. Today there is much doubt about the existence of such all-encompassing leaders within equine society, because according to modern behavioural science no one horse can take this lead position in all facets of life.

Horses are naturally peace-loving animals. Under the care of humans, though, conflicts will occur that are caused by the often constantly changing membership of the herd and the limitations on space.

The effect of stress and domestication on hierarchy

Observations of behaviour relating to social standing when horses are under our care can quickly lead to the wrong conclusions, because a special type of hierarchy can be found in domesticated riding horses that is quite different from that found in horses living in the wild. The frequent integration of new horses as owners and riders change yards means that the animals are being faced repeatedly with having to form new hierarchies within their groupings. At the same time friendships are being torn apart and important social contact is being abruptly brought to an end. These artificially formed equine communities are in sharp contrast to a herd that is formed naturally in the wild and are characterised by a clearly heightened tendency to aggression.

Added to this is the fact that we increase the level of stress by feeding at fixed times in often limited spaces, which results in increased aggression. Contrast this with horses living in the wild with feed that is spread out over a wide area available all day long. Owing to the constant disputes over ranking, our own horses' herds appear to have considerably more potential for conflict. These artificially constructed herds, subject

The degree of aggression shown is less dependent on the horses' ranks within the herd than on the context. Mares with foals at foot assume a special position in the group and will respond more aggressively than mares with no offspring.

to the influence of humans, show a very distorted image of the unspoilt peace-loving nature of horses in the wild.

Situational and contextual dependence

The behaviour of a horse can never be predicted on the basis of its assumed ranking, because the animal's reactions will be decisively influenced by the external situation and its internal psychological state. The entire situational context, and not the ranking alone, decides which risks horses are prepared to take to protect their own interests or whether they will sacrifice certain essential resources. If a lower ranking horse is very thirsty it will be capable of driving a higher ranking horse away from the water trough, at least temporarily. As a result of a specific internal condition – here overwhelming thirst – a horse can react in a manner uncharacteristic of its rank. The readiness of an individual horse to act in a certain way will be influenced significantly by its emotional, physical and mental state, such as how prepared it is to take a potentially risky action, its feeling of thirst or hunger, as well as the influence of life experiences that for a human observer remain a mystery.

This multitude of different elements is what, together with a horse's ranking, influence its behaviour and make the study of the social structure of horses so fascinating. We should avoid viewing horses one-dimensionally, based entirely on the rank they may have within their herd. The term 'hierarchy' often implies a rigid structure within a herd. It would be perhaps more appropriate to think of a herd as a flexible collective. Current scientific studies point more towards a principle of pragmatically rotating roles, in which each animal takes up a specific role based on its own abilities. Each individual carries out a particular job for a limited period. This means that individual animals may have an outstanding talent for a narrow but well defined area of responsibility that they can put to use for the benefit of the entire group and that is recognised by the other members of the herd.

This means that an elderly mare can show the group the best route to take when changing their grazing area thanks to her long years of experience, while a different mare will be able to find and lead the herd to the best waterhole thanks to her well developed sense of smell. In this type of collective society, the harem stallion has the highest rank only when it comes to reproduction, and he fits in with the rest of the members of the community in other areas of life and benefits as all others do from their different abilities. No horse is automatically higher or lower in rank, but in the community each horse assumes an important position at some time thanks to the, perhaps temporary, job that they are carrying out. In this adaptable collective there is neither an alpha nor an omega animal, but only unique and valuable individuals.

Status-related behaviour when hormones come into play

In the course of a year, stallions will have varying levels of the sex hormone testosterone in their blood, which clearly influences their behaviour in relation to their status in the herd. While a lower testosterone level correlates with being less aggressive, a heightened testosterone level will lead to more frequent disputes over issues relating to status. In addition to the seasonal fluctuations that occur, the testosterone level can also fluctuate at very short notice in response to a certain situation, for example to a fight or to danger, and this can make the behaviour of males independent from their ranking. Stallions that live without constant contact with mares often have a very low concentration of testosterone in their blood and are therefore considerably less aggressive than stallions whose testosterone values are permanently increased owing to the presence of the opposite sex. These harem stallions have something to lose and have to be prepared for potential challenges from stallions outside of their group.

In the case of mature mares, the monthly cycle plays a decisive role in status-linked behaviour. A mare that normally has a lower standing can, when she comes into season, attain a higher position owing to the effect of her female sex hormones. These increase her

Scientifically speaking, the concept of a single dominant or subordinate horse is a myth.
In any herd there is neither a single alpha animal nor a clear omega animal.

aggressiveness, because the behaviour linked with her status is governed by her hormones and this is strengthened when she is in season. The balance of hormones is an important and controlling element in the horse. It provides both physical and mental adaptability to the demands of nature and exerts an influence, unseen by us, on the hierarchy amongst horses.

Up and down

If we want to model in more detail the ranking structure within a herd, then we must not just look at the behaviour of a single animal, but must identify the mutual relationship between two horses more precisely. Unfortunately the mistake is all too often made of limiting observation to dominant or status-gaining behaviour.

Status-gaining gestures, including attacking or threatening behaviour, look especially spectacular and are therefore used excessively to assign social status. Using this one-sided way of looking at things we may not be able to identify which animal has the higher ranking, but only to determine the aggressiveness of the two adversaries. In addition, the false impression is given that the relationship between two horses is based primarily on the principle of dominance, in which the will of the stronger animal determines its status.

A much more important component in determining social status is the observation of subservient or status-giving behaviour, such as evasion or getting out of another horse's way, averting the eyes or opening and closing the mouth (as seen in foals). These often very subtle signals are far harder for us to detect, because horses have an astonishing ability to recognise minuscule alterations of facial expressions. From this we can only guess at how delicately structured the communication is between our horses. In our terms, we are talking literally about only a suggestion of a blink, a slight raising of an eyebrow or the gentle pursing of lips.

We should therefore always be aware that only by considering both types of behaviour (status-taking and -giving), which every horse can exhibit, can we truly form a convincing picture of our horses' hierarchical relationships. From a scientific point of view, the principle of there being a single dominant or a clearly subservient horse is a myth.

The concept of friendship

Friendly or cohesive relationships between individual horses develop independently of their social status. Horses form very close friendships that have nothing to do with either age or gender. We recognise befriended horses by the fact that they graze close to each other and will spend most of the day together as a pair. In addition to mutual grooming, you will see them often dozing nose to tail so one can flick away flies from the other's face. These friendships can develop early in life as foals and last a lifetime, and the ranking within the herd of their parents has no influence on how friendships are formed. The only thing that counts is the mutual affection between the animals.

Friendships are the social glue of the herd. The entire connective structure within a herd will be dominated primarily by the interweaving of these bonds of friendship, in which the individuals communicate with each other on the same level and integrate with one another based on the sympathies they feel.

A range of different research has shown that friendship-based behaviour in an established herd is the most common type of behaviour that is seen. Aggressive behaviour is greatly reduced among horses that are cultivating a relationship, even if it is not a firm friendship. In forming the friendship horses give each other the greatest possible space. Naturally formed groups, or those put together skilfully by humans, are characterised by their harmony.

Friendship is the social glue of a herd.

Unfortunately, horse friendships are more often torn apart than nature intended. Perhaps an owner moves away and takes their horse with them, or one half of a pair-bond changes yards because their owner is looking for better hacking. For horses this frequent change is usually a disaster. The animal that is moved away, as well as the one left behind, will suffer from the stress that results from the loss of friendship. Some horses cope with it well and will make new friends easily, while others need months to integrate themselves into a new herd and make friends. Some horses are very choosy when it comes to selecting friends. If in their opinion there is no suitable partner in the new group, they will often remain on the edge with no new partner.

Given that friendships mean a lot to the well-being of every horse, all yard owners should pay great attention to 'mediating' contacts between horses. A horse that is new to a yard should be

allowed to get used to the new surroundings before it is introduced over several weeks to more and more of the group members, so that it can be integrated gradually into the new herd. This is best done when the horses are turned out to grass, because grazing is an enjoyable pastime for all participants, distracts attention from the new group member and will reduce aggressive behaviour. Hacking out together or feeding in sight of others will also increase the feeling of group togetherness. In the rarest of cases a horse may not pair up with any other. Horses are fundamentally very adaptable and will make friends according to the motto 'better you than no one at all'. You will often discover their true preference only when a new and better suited horse enters the group and they drop their previous 'friend' to foster a true partnership with the newcomer.

A state of flux

From the point of view of current behavioural research, a herd of horses consists of a cooperative community of individuals. Every horse has its own role and takes on clearly defined responsibilities for a defined period. Friendships are only formed from mutual affection, meaning that, at pasture, close contact is kept with some horses while others are kept at a distance. Friendships have nothing to do with either the gender or age of the animals. Affection and personal preferences are always dependent on the personality that the horse has been born with, learned patterns of behaviour, internal motivational factors, the hormone levels at the time and on many other parameters about which we have only the vaguest of ideas. Every horse understands its position in relationship to the other herd members, has a certain status, a 'job', a gender-specific role and many further characteristics. In this respect a horse is like a human.

We can wait expectantly on new discoveries from research, but until then we really should throw away the over-simplified model that tries to determine social status based on conflict between horses. A horse's life does not revolve entirely around rank and status, but also around the search for food, defence against enemies and reproduction. Of particular interest in the next few years will be further work by behavioural researchers that involves closer investigation of these equine social networks. It is hoped that particular attention will be paid to the differences among the original different types of horses that date back tens of thousands of years. In nature life is constantly in a state of flux ...

In a horse's life not everything revolves around rank and status.

Understanding communication

How horses communicate
with each other and with us

The body language of horses always pertains to actual events, and the social status of the individual animal can be established from looking at the behaviour of others. A scientifically sound study involves observation of the behaviour of every member of the herd for many hours in a variety of situations and observes each horse in direct contact with every other member of the herd. Each horse will behave according to the situation it is in, which means that it will use its body language so that another horse can read it without misunderstanding. Particularly important spheres that involve status-related body language are the areas that have a particular social meaning among horses. These include greeting rituals, marking of territory, signals to calm situations down, as well as acting to impress mares. The variety of status-related behaviours gives horses and the watchful observer information about the complex network that exists within a group of horses.

During ritualised fighting serious injury is usually avoided. The well rehearsed moves in fights such as these between animals of the same species serve to prevent harm on either side.

Horses among themselves

Aggressive behaviour amongst horses is often exhibited through a form of ritual fighting. A ritualised fight is a strictly regimented form of fighting between opponents of the same species. Two stallions usually settle differences of opinion like this. A signal from one will be followed by a responding signal from the other. The movements are so embedded in their behaviour that they serve the purpose of solving out a dispute without seriously injuring either of them. Neither of the horses intends to wound the other fatally. Particularly well known ritualised movements include circling one another, nipping the foreleg of the opponent to force him onto his knees, rearing up opposite each other and snapping at the head. The difference in status between the two horses will become clear during the ritual fight through the degree to which the various types of 'display' behavioural patterns are shown by the opponents.

Macho stallion?

The behaviour of a horse is described as 'display' behaviour when it serves the purpose of showing its own strengths to another without actually having to start a fight. The opponents will assess each other and then decide whether it is worth fighting. A potential mate will base part of its decision about whether or not it is looking at an attractive partner on the sexual display behaviour shown.

The best known types of display behaviour include a stallion gathering himself up and arching his neck and the elevated passage-like trot in slow motion. How these moves are expressed and the degree to which they are developed in a horse

will depend on its personality, type and breed. Some horses are more extroverted and others calmer in displaying this behaviour. Many trainers assume that stallions with a strong tendency to display these patterns of behaviour are automatically 'dominant' stallions. This link doesn't exist. The display patterns of a stallion may be shown more or less strongly depending on its sexual interest, hormone status and motivation. A stallion who shows off these ritual moves isn't dominant per se, but is sexually interested. Punishing a horse that shows these sexual needs can result in serious psychological problems. Typical problem behaviour in stallions can be found when the animals are kept in poor conditions, whether the stallion is with a herd or kept as a lone individual. For this reason you should distance yourself from methods that could label a stallion as dominant and therefore dangerous, or that would punish his natural behaviour rather than trying to steer him down a better track without the use of force.

Stallion-like behaviour in geldings

The way we keep our horses means that we don't often see stallions, or the way they behave naturally, but instead we see many more geldings. A gelding's behaviour is usually quieter and the degree to which they show sexually motivated behaviour, both in frequency and intensity, is substantially lower. Despite this, geldings are still male animals whose sexual behaviour, depending on when castration took place, remains in a youthful stage of development. For this reason many of the insights that biologists have collected from research on wild stallions can be applied to geldings living under typical modern management systems. Groups of geldings can be compared easily to groups of bachelors in the wild. Here too there is a very fluid intertwining of rank, easy friendships and a great tendency to play around together. In mixed groups a gelding will often form a firm friendship with a mare, gently wooing her as a stallion would. Of course the display behaviour is less well developed, and covering occurs rarely, but there is little difference seen in the affection towards the mare. A gelding that was castrated late may even mark the mare's droppings with its own. In general, the later they are castrated, the more likely a gelding is to show stallion-like behaviour.

The display behaviour shown by stallions is often sexually motivated and is not necessarily a sign of dominance.

Greeting rituals between horses

Horses greet each other in a different manner from the way in which they greet people. A horse that is introduced into a new group does not automatically know which horse has which position in the herd; it doesn't yet understand the group's social maze and has first of all to find its way around. The greeting ritual serves primarily to reduce the potential for violence. It avoids escalation of a delicate situation and enables the horses to get to know one another carefully. Two animals meeting for the first time will sniff each other's nostrils. Here the individual scent of a horse is the strongest, and could almost be compared to a business card. Distance is often maintained from strange horses by squealing and stamping the foreleg. More experienced horses are often very calm and superior when meeting new horses because they don't easily become threatened.

The reasons stallions mark their territory

For horses it is very important for their social standing that they mark their territory. Stallions and late-castrated geldings will cover the droppings of their mares with their own droppings. By doing this they are clearly demonstrating to other males their rights over these mares. As clear as this form of communication may be to other horses, for us this type of behaviour can appear strange and difficult to understand. This aspect of creating a herd's hierarchy takes place quietly and unspectacularly and research requires a skilled observer and careful analysis of how the various piles of droppings are constituted.

Signs of appeasement

Of particular importance in the rank-based communication system that exists among horses are the signs of appeasement or

Turning its gaze away is a typical calming signal for a horse.
It serves to diffuse a potentially dangerous situation.

soothing, described collectively as 'calming signals'. Using these signals horses express their own stress and indicate their willingness for conciliation. Licking and chewing, conspicuous and frequent yawning that has nothing to do with tiredness, or a slight turning away of the entire body, are some of the best known calming signals.

These signals serve to diffuse a situation and help horses to development harmonious and lasting relationships more peacefully. A horse will often show these signals towards a horse that has a higher social status, so these signs of body language can be used to work out a rough idea of the structure of a herd.

Independent of social status, mutual grooming is an expression of affection between two horses and creates trust and a feeling of wellbeing.

Mutually grooming their way towards friendship

Two pair-bonded horses aren't just caring for each other's coats and skin when scratching each other along the mane, back and at the top of the tail. Mutual grooming is one of the most important acts for cementing the relationship between two horses and serves to deepen the peaceful nature of the community's structure. It is an indicator of the strongest bond within an equine family – friendship. Mutual grooming expresses the affection that two horses have for each other, regardless of what rank they may have. Horses are divorced from their social status when it comes to a close friend. A horse that has higher standing in the herd than another can demand that a lower ranked horse scratches an itch for it, but there is no rule that says who starts and who finishes. It appears more to be a mutual give and take. Scratching one another creates trust and improves wellbeing. The heart rate of the horse doing the scratching slows, so the act

The best way of developing effective communication between you and your horse is by learning a mutual form of sign language.

of scratching becomes a valuable stress-relieving factor.

Horse and human in conversation

Communication between horses differs in several essential ways from communication between horse and human. First of all, both species have a different basis for what they want to communicate and the way they express themselves.

Horses communicate with each other to exchange information, to tell others about their own feelings, to underpin the social structure and to avoid danger. To do this they have a very carefully designed repertoire of gestures, expressions and body language. Any alteration of a single part of the body has a meaning for another horse. Horses have the ability to distinguish the faintest of movements of even less than a millimetre. Even the blinking of another horse's eye potentially means something. The more obvious parts of body language are the posture, the muscle tone (tensed

At first glance this pony looks friendly with his ears pricked; however the minuscule signals shown around his mouth reveal his inner tension.

or relaxed) and the position of the body, head and neck. In addition there are the various states of the body such as the breathing rate, muscle twitching and veins standing out. The subtleties of body language lie in the microscopic signs – the slightest of alterations in the expression of the eyes or the way the lips or nostrils are moved. With all the potential that its body language has, the horse is far superior in many respects to the human.

We are not in a position to move our ears around like a horse. We stand on two legs and this significantly changes the way that we can use our body to express ourselves. In addition, our eyes are positioned differently on our head and we lack a tail to show what sort of mood we are in. In short, our communication is based on a different way of expressing ourselves and our body language is human. Of course there are similarities in body language shared by human and horse. When excited or scared both species will move differently and may begin to sweat. In humans, a change in breathing is a good indication of a change in mood. However the differences are really in the detail. Horses, like people, may be able to learn some of the language of the other species, but much will still stay hidden.

To develop a workable dialogue with horses it is important to give them, from as young an age as possible, the opportunity to learn the language of humans. However, we will always run up against our own limitations in being able to transmit what we want to say, owing to the physical impossibility of using the same sort of expressions that a horse has at its disposal. One alternative to a communication system based purely on the physical lies in developing a shared sign language. Horses are very intelligent creatures that, through the use of reward, can be encouraged to use their abilities to notice the smallest of changes. This is the key to communicating with horses.

Resource management

We are in a position to control the life and education of our horses by managing the resources that are essential to our horses appropriately. By resources, I mean the variety of things that are essential for our horse's existence. One resource, for example, is feed, but another important requirement could also be a mate. We control all of these resources and make them available as appropriate to the horses we look after. Horses are very skilled at recognising how to get things they want and who is responsible for providing them. In terms of feed alone, we are a significant controller of one of the most important resources. The horse will draw its own conclusions from this and will be prepared to work with us in order to access these resources. The type of resource management that is linked to certain situations in life, together with the knowledge of how a horse learns, opens up to us the possibility of utilising this learning behaviour to our ends rather than having to deal with the question of rank or hierarchy.

Peaceful coexistence

In order to be able to live in harmony with horses, we need to remind ourselves why horses exhibit hierarchical behaviour. What is their motivation? A hierarchy serves to avoid conflict and reduce aggression within a group. Horses feel better when they can determine the preferences and dislikes, and the abilities and shortcomings, of their companions. The herd can live in peace when the positions within the herd are clear.

Only when a horse knows its position within the herd or sees a particular resource put at risk will it show behaviour that is related to its status within the herd. The most important catalyst for this is competition for status within the herd. Given that the natural possibilities for feeding or for reproduction are limited, it will come down to a matter of competition with others of the same species. Horses try to secure the best conditions for themselves and their offspring, using a variety of strategies in order to be able to pass on their genes successfully to the next generation. A good social standing secures certain advantages for an individual and survival for its group.

This inevitably poses the question of whether we humans can be in competition with our horses. We don't live within the same community but we come into it as a visitor and are usually engaged with a single horse and not with the entire group. We don't use the same body language or express ourselves in the same way. We don't eat the same things and we are not in competition for the same mates. Those of us who have compared how a horse greets another horse for the first time with the way it greets an unknown person will understand that horses know that we are not a horse, but something else. They obviously don't see us as a part of their community, and therefore the rules that apply to us are different from those that govern members of a herd. By definition, a hierarchy represents the structure of a group whose members stand in competition with one another. This doesn't apply to the combination of horse and human. Scientifically speaking it is incorrect to use the terms hierarchy, dominance or herd in relation to the relationship between horse and human. A horse can of course form a relationship with its owner or rider, but we will never be integrated into the structure of the herd and instead will have a special role assigned to us.

Nature gives every species an ecological niche that defines its preferences for its sources of food, climate, environmental conditions and surroundings. In other words it gives a species its vocation in the life cycle of the planet. As a large herbivore, the horse has an important position in relation to its forage plants, its predators and also the parasites that live off it, just as humans fulfil a different position in nature. These cycles will intersect, as it were, when a human decides to keep a horse. When living by themselves in the wild every horse has a particular role, i.e. a social niche that it occupies. In the intersection that occurs when a relationship forms between you and your horse, you must try to establish a social niche or a connection between two different living beings outside of the normal conventions of the two species.

You can never become a full member of your horse's herd because it is capable of distinguishing a horse from a human. Despite this you can still become a friend, albeit on a non-equine basis.

The myth of dominance

Dominance training in the light of behavioural science

Behavioural researchers discovered the first simple hierarchies in a variety of animal species at the beginning of the twentieth century. Once the same patterns of behaviour had been looked for among horses the fate of dominance theory in horse training started to run its course. Regardless of later discoveries and developing knowledge, popular methods of training were established using the principle of a herd's social structure. Depending on the trends prevailing at the time, different models emerged: the 'lead stallion' model, the 'lead mare' principle, or a system of a dominant form of body language. All of these trends assumed that a person could take up a level of social standing within a group of horses and create respect by showing 'dominant' behaviour. The dominant person would make all the decisions for their horse, and in turn the horse would obey them unquestioningly. The methods used to achieve this vary, but they have certain similarities, such as the concept of pressure and release, by which the horse has to decide between two unpleasant choices – to give in to pressure or to avoid it.

Humankind – a worthy alpha animal?

Sensitive horses will quickly notice what abilities the person standing opposite them has and what they are obviously lacking.

Seeing potential dangers, for example, isn't among the talents of most humans, because they have a limited field of vision. This is, however, a particularly important ability for someone in a position of leadership within equine society. Even if there could be

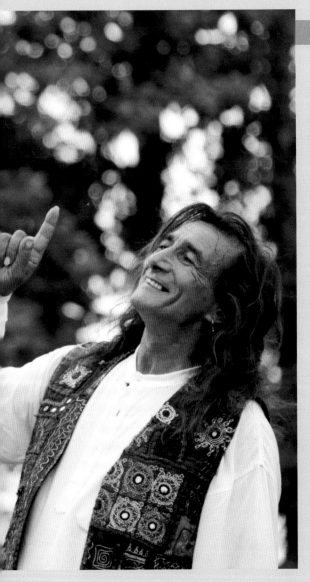

Good communication has nothing to do with social status.

repertoire of body signals. We are not able to imitate any of them successfully, and so we are also unable to answer any questions relating to dominance because we can't make ourselves understood by the horse. Even if we were somehow able to establish ourselves as the lead or alpha animal, we would not be able to exert any control over a horse. Hierarchies have nothing to do with learning or giving orders. Even if we were the king of the herd, our horse would still not be able to do better flying changes. One has nothing to do with the other. Similarly, horses will only learn in connection with their own experiences and not because of social status. In addition, horses are no less dangerous or more obedient to humans just because people behave in a dominant manner towards them. Conscious learning is always an active process that requires an understanding of the things that are being learnt. You can't drum the required behaviour into a horse or order it to do something because you think that you are more dominant. In order to understand these general principles of learning better, we need to look more closely at how a horse learns.

Dominance training vs learning theory

a shared hierarchy between two different species, in the eyes of a horse we would be unlikely to look like a born leader, but rather because of our physical insufficiencies we would more likely be at the opposite end of the scale. Horses communicate with each other using a very clearly differentiated

The two competing camps in horse training advance two fundamentally different explanations for their theories. The followers of dominance theory maintain that horses, once they have accepted a person as being higher 'ranked' than them, will henceforth follow all orders without

Nothing happens without motivation. A horse that is forced to do something will never do it of its own volition.

contradiction. Followers of learning theory, on the other hand, keep to the scientific fact that good behaviour and carrying out practised exercises is down to motivation and learning.

From a scientific perspective any learned behaviour is based on modern learning theory. Thus the followers of dominance theory are also drawing from this pot, it's just that they use pressure and then dress it up with pretty-sounding descriptions. This phenomenon occurs, for example, when a trainer says during a demonstration that they are moving into a horse's space, like a dominant mare in a herd would, 'so that the horse learns to respect their position'. By this they mean that they are putting the horse under pressure to

cause a reaction. The most important principle of learning behaviour is that learning takes place constantly and can't be turned on and off as needed. A horse is aware of its environment and adapts itself to its circumstances. It learns especially from the consequences of its own behaviour and from the emotions derived from them. Behaviour that is worthwhile or has been rewarded in the past will be shown more often. Correspondingly, behaviour that is not worthwhile will be shown less often in the future. It is the horse that decides what is worthwhile behaviour and what is not, rather than the person.

For example, people may think that they are punishing a behaviour by shouting to discourage a horse from doing it again. From a human perspective, we don't like being told off. A horse, on the other hand, may be looking for the attention that it then receives in plenty. Its behaviour becomes very worthwhile for it at this level and won't be reduced, but on the contrary is likely to become more frequent. We must therefore always pay careful attention to what our horse's motivation may be and what the reasons for a specific action are.

In order to understand a horse's motivation and the various possibilities for learning, we must look more closely at how horses learn. There are a variety of ways in which horses learn, some of which take place in parallel and are inseparable from each other. I would like to introduce these briefly in the following section.

Habituation

Using habituation as a learning process means that nothing new is learnt, but that something is forgotten, namely the reaction to a particular sensory perception or stimulus. A horse will probably get a fright when it sees someone putting up an umbrella for the first time. If this is action is repeated often enough, and there are neither positive nor negative consequences for the horse as a result of the action, then its reaction to the umbrella is likely to get less and less until there may be no reaction at all. However, it will continue to react strongly to other scary things because its instinct to take flight will not be so easily forgotten, and for good reason.

This type of learning is commonly used in horse training. Young horses will often be put to graze in fields near busy roads so that from the safety of their field they will have neither negative or positive experiences with vehicles. They become

In training for calmness, horses are habituated step by step to unusual stimuli, so that they don't show fear.

accustomed to the noise of the traffic insidiously. This process isn't very effective, however, unless the stimulation (in this example the noise of traffic) takes place often enough.

If a stimulus is very strong or painful, or causes the horse to be afraid, then we get to the next learning process, sensitisation.

Sensitisation

In this type of learning the horse will become more sensitive to a specific stimulus. Many trainers, including the advocates of dominance theory, make use of this learning mechanism to, for example, get the horse to react faster to the swinging of a rope or to a person's threatening body language. Using this method, it is intended that a horse will perceive an unaccustomed movement or the body language of the person as a threat and will react with fear to the stimulus, which it will try to get away from. The horse learns through negative experience and will become more and more sensitive to the stimulus, for example a rope. The word sensitisation sounds positive but in terms of behavioural science it has no clear positive meaning, but rather a neutral one. Although we say that the horse reacts more sensitively to a stimulus, we can't say anything about whether they like doing so or not.

Imprinting and socialisation

Imprinting refers to a collection of learning processes that are limited to a period of time during the very sensitive phase of a foal's early life. One example is the imprinting on the foal's mother. The result is very fixed. However, if foals are restricted in this early learning experience, or disturbed during it, behavioural problems can result.

In addition there is a phase of socialisation in which young horses will approach new things without inhibitions and will learn to find their way about the world of the horse and human. They don't consciously 'learn' to do this but do it automatically. This sociali-sation phase is a window that stays open for a limited period of time as set down by nature. In terms of a foal identifying itself as a horse, this lasts until the foal is approximately 43 days old, and then there is an additional window of time that lasts until the 84th day during which the foal can learn to relate to humans or to other species. A foal should therefore at this age have learned to be able to trust us as partners.

Imitation or social stimulation

By definition, learning only takes place through imitation when a horse does something purely as a result of having observed another individual doing it and without having been able to do it before. This true 'learning from watching' process is actually very rare and the learning is often more likely to be the result of chance.

The horse also has access to a more widespread mechanism of social learning, which is imitation. Here the foal may copy an adult horse that is grazing, without understanding why the other is dropping its head down to the ground so strangely. It is only by doing it itself that the foal learns it can eat the grass and that this is essential for survival. Horses learn many other things through watching, but researching this field of learning has proven to be extremely difficult.

Classical conditioning

Every horse owner observes this type of learning at feeding time. Horses will react with excitement to the sound of the feed bin being opened, because they associate the noise with the event of being fed. During

The herd is the ideal nursery during the most important phase of socialisation.
Only here can a foal really gain self-confidence.

classical conditioning, what was originally a neutral stimulus acquires a specific meaning and the horse's brain will make an unconscious association between two events.

Operant conditioning

Operant conditioning allows the modification of behaviour as a result of its consequences. In other words, it can be described as learning by trial and error. The horse tries a number of different possibilities in a new situation and, depending on the positive or negative experience, will draw its own conclusions. In this way it learns a new behaviour voluntarily and deliberately. Operant conditioning is heavily dependent on the horse's motivation, its current mood and its individual readiness to learn. A trainer must therefore consider why a horse would want to do something at all. These reasons could include pleasure for the horse, and this may convince a horse to display a certain behaviour through gentle persuasion. The reasons could, however, be more negative in nature and more or less subtly force a horse to do something.

In principle we have four ways
of influencing our horses' behaviour:

1. We can do something our horse finds unpleasant (i.e. punish it)
2. We can stop doing something that our
   horse doesn't like (end a punishment)
3. We can give the animal something it will
   like (give a reward)
4. We can stop doing something the horse
   likes (take a reward away).

In order to recognise what our own training methods are, we need to allocate them
to one of these four options. The green zone
represents the non-forceful spectrum of
learning by reward. The closer we get to the
red area, which involves methods using
pressure, then the less non-forceful the
training method is.

Training options

When working with horses you have four methods to choose from. You could ...

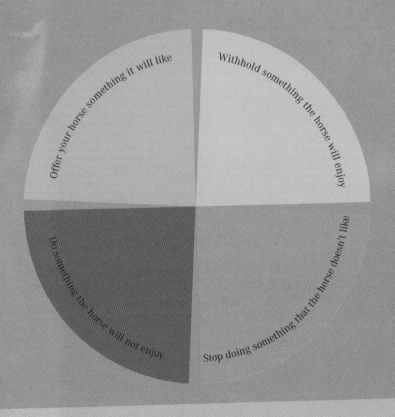

Offer your horse something it will like

Withhold something the horse will enjoy

Do something the horse will not enjoy

Stop doing something that the horse doesn't like

We have a choice: do we want to force a horse to do something or motivate it using a system of rewards?

When speaking of these possibilities, they can be described as positive and negative punishment as well as positive and negative reinforcement. Regardless of the fact that, from a scientific perspective, there are four possible ways to exert an influence, the followers of the dominance theory work almost exclusively using negative reinforcement and with punishment. These trainers wait for a horse to show a certain behaviour that at that moment is not desired and correct its behaviour by using a negative response. Or they cause a horse to do something by using pressure even

when the horse doesn't really want to and doesn't enjoy doing it.

Followers of the dominance theory train their horses according to the principle of pressure and release. The pressure is gradually built up until the horse shows a reaction. Then the pressure is immediately released – at least in the case of professional trainers. The release of pressure or a break is the only 'reward' that the horse gets. In the case of training in a round pen the horse is rewarded by the trainer ceasing to drive the horse forwards with a rope when they show some cooperation, and the horse will be punished by being driven forwards again if it reacts too slowly. According to the definition from the field of behavioural science, there is no true reward, because the horse isn't given something positive, but rather there is just a withdrawal of the punishment. This is a huge difference not just for the person training but also for the horse being trained. Horses trained like this don't respond because they enjoy doing it, but rather because they are afraid of the consequences if they don't. They choose the lesser evil and become an animal that takes orders without the ability to have its own say.

These methods are associated with a number of disadvantages. Horses trained like this actually receive only limited information about what the point of the training is. They mainly learn what they can and can't do. This type of learning will often over a longer term cause the horse to become frustrated and its behaviour will become subdued. The horse may appear to be well behaved and uncomplicated but it is likely to have lost any enjoyment in its work or its inter-action with people – a high price to pay for obedience. In the longer term the rela-tionship between horse and rider can be permanently damaged. A training system that is based exclusively on negatives, with only short breaks as rewards, will cause the horse to become stressed. It is very difficult to learn when under stress, so any real progress will be very slow. As harmless as the use of psycho-pressure may sound, its effects are devastating for the psychological wellbeing of a horse.

Carrot and more stick?

Essentially, the methods described previously will only work if the trainer is fundamentally prepared to exert pressure on the horse, keep it up and if necessary increase it. Fatally for this method, a horse will get used to the degree of pressure so that gradually more and more is required in order to achieve the desired results – to a point where a trainer may sometimes be seen to lose their temper.

This poses the question of how far any of us is prepared to go in forcing a horse to do what we want. In the case of sensitive or frightened horses we may get the desired reaction by using the obligatory waving of the rope or aggressive body language. How-ever, in the case of less sensitive horses, a lot more pressure will be needed, possibly involving hitting the horse with either a whip or the end of the rope. How are we then going to increase the pressure? Do we really want to increase the pressure further? At some time all of us will reach a point when we know that we can't go any further. For some a slap with a whip is too much; for someone else, though, that point is only reached when they use a twitch and or a device to give the horse an electric shock.

Regardless of where someone's individ-ual pain barrier is, the problem lies in the principle behind the method. Anyone who has decided to use a method of training that uses negative reinforcement and phases in increased levels of pressure must be pre-pared to step over that line in order to increase the pressure even more. Otherwise this training method will not work. Most of us who like horses instinctively would not

Good riding is possible without pressure! Even unspectacular horses gain greatly in expression when ridden like this.

want to do this. Many riders might feel that these pressurising methods aren't morally correct but will be convinced by professional instructors of their necessity. These trainers use very measured and subtle pressure and are often unscrupulous enough to raise the pressure considerably. Their horses apparently 'function' perfectly. This impresses many riders and convinces them to imitate the methods used by these trainers.

However one look into the empty and lifeless eyes of these horses reveals at what cost this method of pressure and release works: it is at the cost of the horse's love of life and its personality. At the same time the risks posed to the unpractised or inexperienced handler will be totally forgotten. Every animal will accept a certain degree of pressure uncomplainingly. It may work quite well for a long time, but at some stage it will look for a way out of the situation. In the best case it might not let itself be caught and brought in from the field. In the worst case it may try to strike back and become aggressive. At some stage the horse will feel that it has nothing to lose. If a horse trained in this manner is pushed into a

corner, physically or mentally, by an apparently harmless command then it may literally try and fight for its life. These counter-attacks can be totally unexpected.

Many people who work according to the principle of pressure and release forget somehow that they are exerting a potentially crippling pressure with this training method. They make the pauses and the release of pressure sound positive. But the reality is that you can only stop doing something that you have at some stage started. You can't reduce or take off pressure where there is none to start with. This gradual build-up of pressure is a punishment for the horse in behavioural science terms, no matter how little pressure there may be.

The principle itself has a negative connotation and represents a form of punishment to which a horse reacts with negative physical reactions, avoidance or evasion behaviour while showing fear, annoyance or stress. Many of the exercises promoted by supporters of the dominance theory work by the use of this mechanism of reaction. The learning process itself is a form of conditioned response that is created by largely negative effects. The horse learns how to avoid the pressure but not always much about the dominance of the trainer. There are no signs that the horse recognises the dominance of the trainer, but it is only the potential for aggression towards the horse that is revealed. According to the concept of 'pressure and release', the only thing that horses learn at all costs is to avoid the trainer's gaze or their swinging rope.

Learning by reward

Horses can also be taught to be our reliable partners without using the methods of the supporters of dominance if you know how to motivate them positively. Here the focus is placed on behaviour shown by a horse that by chance happens to be 'correct' in terms of what we want. This is immediately rewarded with praise, attention, gentle rubbing or treats. Given that a horse will exhibit behaviour more when it is something that is worthwhile doing, it can be trained gradually into a happy and obedient partner. When this happens, the horse is rewarded immediately with praise, attention, petting or treats.

The use of rewards means that the horse will have more motivation to do things for you. The horse will seek out the company of people and will want to do the exercises. By using praise and rewards we are able to show clearly when something is right. We are giving clear and full instructions because the horse no longer has to try out different variations but learns from the start which reaction is being sought to earn the reward. This method is called positive reinforcement. It is used in a variety of modern training methods including the very effective clicker training, which has been developed on the basis of learning theory.

The change from dominance training to learning by reward

It is never too late for you to look for a different way of working together with your horse. Horses have the ability to learn into old age and are always able to learn new reactions or associations. A

Little gifts help you stay friends!

change in method can have advantages for horses. While classical dominance training can have a demotivating and restricting effect, learning by reward allows the horse to experience its own creativity and enjoyment of life, giving it the chance to work with its trainer in an environment free of stress.

Usually it is the humans that have more problems implementing this change, because they have often only ridden or trained horses using methods associated with dominance training. It requires a lot of courage and hard work to change to a different training method because we must change our attitudes and put old habits aside. However, this step from dominance training to learning by reward will lead the human-horse partnership into a new relationship based on friendship. As soon as we begin to motivate our horses positively, we will be rewarded by their enthusiasm and a new light in their eyes.

Risks and side-effects

Having outlined some of my thoughts on training methods in general, using examples from the area of dominance training, I would like to make you aware of some of the risks that can accompany these methods. I will refer to some well known methods but with the knowledge that some trainers may do it differently. I will be concentrating mainly on the behavioural aspects and question whether what happens under the guise of theory and clever terminology is really what those using pressure-related methods do in practice, or whether from a behavioural

research point of view it is all just clever packaging. Furthermore I would like to mention some of the risks that many of the supporters of these methods are keen to keep quiet about and also the effects on the horse's psychological and physical wellbeing.

Imprint training

Labelled as a pioneering method for the education of newborn foals, imprint training spread from America to Europe some years ago. According to this theory, the newborn foal should be touched all over its body immediately after birth and held until it shows no more signs of resistance. In addition, to prepare it for being ridden it is desensitised to being touched in certain important areas. This is done by touching the foal in the mouth where the bit will later be positioned, or by putting increasing pressure on the girth area until it reacts by moving away. All of this should result in a particularly obedient horse and nip any of the usual problems encountered in the bud – or that's the theory!

In practice, however, it can be quite different. On the one hand those who advocate this method claim that the process of imprinting is a natural process. In reality though, this process can be hugely disruptive to the natural process of the foal imprinting on its mother. Holding an animal against its will is just as much a form of violence as hitting it. A flood of stimuli is also created, the danger of which we will examine in more detail later. A young horse is completely overwhelmed with impressions, and this is used by us in order to demonstrate our superiority. In doing this we are stepping between a mother and

Foals need companions of the same age to play with in order to learn how to form friendships and to be able to develop a secure equine personality.

her offspring when they are at a crucial stage of forging their relationship. This can result in an imprinting error that can become an identity crisis whereby the foal doesn't see itself as a horse. Possible results are a deep sense of insecurity, trauma or even a state of shock. This all happens in the attempt to create a perfectly functioning riding horse. Horses are not puppets, but instead have a right to develop their personality in a normal and healthy way and not have this process interfered with.

Round pen training

A well known method of training that is based on the principles of dominance theory is what is known as round pen training. This involves

The right way to imprint: approaching a foal carefully during the sensitive early phase using gentle forms of physical contact will encourage a positive relationship with humans. Compare this with the more common method of imprinting which can overwhelm a young horse.

introducing the horse to a circular lungeing arena with a high fence, with the trainer standing in the middle asking the horse to move around him. The person in the middle secures their position of dominance and after a certain time the horse should voluntarily 'join up' with the person.

In reality this method also uses the principle of pressure and release. The trainer exerts more or less pressure on the horse, depending on its sensitivity, until the horse reacts by moving. Owing to the circular nature of the round pen and the high surrounding fence the horse cannot get away. Eventually it recognises that there is no escape and that it will only be left in peace when it unconditionally follows the commands given, because any other behaviour will lead to it being chased off around the arena again. There is, however, no alteration in terms of the dominance of the handler. In reality the characteristics that the trainer takes as a sign of the horse recognising their authority (dropping the head, licking and chewing) can, from a behavioural science perspective, be attributed to the stress and the powerlessness caused by the pressure during the training.

Natural horsemanship

There is a further series of methods that function according to the aforementioned principle of 'pressure and release' and are apparently aimed at improving the handler's social status in the 'herd'. They can be referred to collectively under the term 'natural horsemanship'. Some trainers work accordingly to a well developed series of steps, with units that are built one on top of the other and use special lead ropes, halters and whips.

All these methods use an increase of pressure to cause the horse to react. In the case of professional trainers, when a reaction is shown the pressure is removed immediately. The horse therefore learns from negative reinforcement that doing what the handler asks is inevitable. The horse is directed by the handler's body language or the other aids, with disobedience of a command resulting in the next stage of pressure being introduced. It learns to do what it is asked not because it trusts the trainer or because it is

True horsemanship in the best sense of the word means cooperation without pressure or violence.

enjoying doing it, but rather to avoid an unpleasant stimulus. The supposed harmlessness and non-forceful nature of this method frequently appeals to the unsuspecting horse owner.

What does learned helplessness mean?

If a horse finds that it is subjected to excessive or inconsistent punishment, then alongside fear and aggression, a state that is known as learned helplessness may also develop. The horse will act more and more passively, and when the condition is particularly strongly developed the horse will not try to resist at all but just submit to its fate. It is similar to some forms of depression found in people.

The horse perceives that its needs are not being met and its feelings are not being respected, and that it can neither resist nor escape. A horse that has reached this state can be recognised by the absence of ear play, when the ears flick back and forth to show its attention shifting from one point to another, and by the inward-looking gaze and general lacklustre expression. Such horses are often held up by their trainers to be particularly well behaved and well trained and by many owners are seen as being absolutely normal. The horse has learned that it isn't worth trying out anything and behaves as passively and inconspicuous as possible. In reality these poor animals are totally oppressed and live in a state of constant stress and fear. We are dealing here with animals that deserve pity, and that have in effect cut themselves off from their feelings in order to be able to survive. A horse affected like this is suffering a form of psychological torture.

It is precisely this state, however, that seems to be the desired result in many of the training systems that work using the principles of dominance theory, even if the trainer would probably not describe it like this. Only a weak-willed, obedient and well behaved horse is apparently a good one. What is totally forgotten along the way is that a horse has a soul that can be only too easily destroyed when treated like this. The controversial and much debated use of hyperflexion also trains the horse systematically into a state of learned helplessness. The horse is taught that there is no point in trying to evade the rider, because the rider is superior whatever the position. In addition, the field of vision is considerably limited and so the horse is more reliant on the rider to give it direction.

Learned helplessness and the accompanying passivity should never be considered desirable or good. On the contrary, people should pay more attention and should not use trainers whose horses give the impression of having reached a state of learned helplessness. The world of competition and its governing bodies should also pay more

The sad eyes, the lack of ear play and the resigned expression are all clear signs of learned helplessness.

attention to the silent suffering of these animals. Only by working together for the good of the horse can we end this type of psychological violence.

Without force – or perhaps not?

The terms 'without force' and 'without violence' are greatly over-used in the world of training horses, and especially in the world of dominance training where they appear to be a generally recognised feature. Whether a method involves force or not is a definition set by the individual. For one person, avoiding the use of physical force may be enough; another might go one step further. In the case of many traditional riding instructors, as well as with the modern American and Dutch systems of training, the psychological force that is used on horses should not be underestimated. What is non-violent to the trainer is not necessarily the same to the horse.

The question of what a horse feels during a training session can only be answered by the horse. We should always pay attention to whether the horse is really enjoying its work – in other words whether they show enthusiasm in their movement and a happy expression, and whether it has watchful eyes and ears that move frequently. All these will help you to decide whether a method is using force or not. A horse that appears passive or numb and shows fear or apprehension is not enjoying its work and won't see training as enjoyable or as something that does not involve force.

It is also not necessary for a horse to be drenched in sweat or to be agitated for them to learn something new. When selecting a trainer the methods used should be seen not only at demonstrations but most especially during their day to day work, in order for you to be able to decide whether or not they rely on force and whether the methods will work for you and your horse. Horses that are put under too much pressure at home may work well in public because of the fear they have for their trainer. At moments like this many methods appear less forceful than they really are when practised at home.

As we would like to be treated ourselves ...

When choosing a training method it is always helpful to ask whether we would be happy to take the place of our horse. Before an exercise the horse doesn't know what it is going to do or why it is doing it. Many riders are heavily influenced by the apparent tradition behind dominance theory and by its many advocates. They perceive techniques and actions as normal that an outsider would never class as such.

They way we deal with our horses is not always guided by common sense, but instead and rather too often we religiously follow the big names, the latest in fashionable training methods and the current training gurus. In return for the appropriate reimbursement, some resourceful business people promise their customers a horse that 'works perfectly'. What you are not told is that its personality will be lost. Many of these methods don't care about the horse but focus on the comfort and the confidence of the owner. The models these trainers use to explain what they are doing do not follow the principles of behavioural science, but rather use its vocabulary to demonstrate the apparently natural nature of the methods and to justify the negative actions with pseudo-science.

Clever terminology

Dominance training is characterised by the often flowery language used to describe the processes, the purported scientific background, the equipment, or simply the image of the method. These euphemisms are cleverly used to market the training concepts as being free of force. Terms such as 'playing', 'lead mare principle', or 'touching' are used to give a person a better feeling when carrying out the chosen methods. Whether these terms live up to the promises and whether they can be classified as being correct in terms of behavioural science will only be revealed by closer examination.

Many of these theories can be checked against the criteria of learning theory, by looking objectively at exactly what the trainer does and how they describe the processes they are using. In general there are only four ways, which we have already described, to train horses. Either you build up pressure and then release it, or you offer or withhold a reward. These principles of learning are universal and no trainer in the world can ignore them for the benefit of dominance training. If a horse reacts passively, fearfully, particularly nervously or is tense, then you can assume that negative reinforcement has been used in training. The way a horse behaves, its facial expressions and the overall impression the horse gives tell us how it has been or is being trained.

As long as people see their horses as pieces of sports equipment that have to work perfectly, they will continue only to consider performance and to rob their horses of their personalities.

You can check your own methods by cutting back on the aids used. Often certain aids or commands lose their positive meaning and have to be revealed for what they really are. Thus a supposedly harmless stick is nothing other than

Whether in a circus or in a show, only a look behind the scenes will show the truth about the training methods used.

a type of whip that also serves to build up pressure.

You must also be cautious when watching professionals during performances. Not everything that is shown or wrapped up in pretty language or clever terminology is actually free of force. Horses that work apparently at liberty, in other words without reins, whip or spurs, are often trained using methods based on negative pressure. They work well because they are conditioned to carry out the required movements, but they often fear punishment if they don't obey. In the case of shows, the expression of the horse can be covered up by the horse's natural excitement. It is always best to observe a trainer and their methods at home in famil-iar surroundings.

In the following section I would like to address some of the common terminology used by followers of dominance theory and clarify what lies behind it.

Dominance training

The use of the words 'dominance training' is often a misuse of a term that comes from behavioural science. It isn't possible to create dominance through training. In a herd of horses there are no overall dominant animals. The term 'dominant' refers only to the difference in behaviour between two individuals within a certain context or situation. What is actually being done is dressing up a scientific term and giving it to a training programme that is based on pressure. From a behavioural science perspective the result of dominance training isn't that the trainer reaches a position of leadership, but rather that the horse reaches a state of learned helplessness, during which it totally gives up its own initiative, stops trying things for itself and passively endures the actions of the trainer.

Everything is 'natural'

There is an increased trend to refer collectively to so much in horse training as being 'natural' in order to justify using characteristics of the horse's own nature in the methods. Given that we turn to other aids even when using these so-called 'natural' methods, however, you can't really refer to it as a truly natural type of communication. If these methods really followed natural mechanisms of communication, then we wouldn't need ropes, sticks or round pens to reinforcement our arguments.

Numerous terms can be used - for example touching, driving, contact or tugging - all of which are supposed to justify the use of pressure under the cover of forming a new pecking order. It would be more honest to describe what is really being done: touching with a whip is and will always be hitting; driving a horse away in a round pen can also be described as chasing. It's not what you say but the way you say it. Without the euphemisms the actions and methods used by some trainers suddenly don't seem to be quite as harmless.

Body language

Entire books have been written about body language. Here too the use of the term in behavioural science has been undermined by definitions that can be misleading. In the herd, horses can pick up very subtle signals given through body language, which is why they could theoretically also learn to interpret human body language. This process would have to have taken place during the horse's socialisation phase, however, and this type of learning can't be repeated at a later stage in life. For most horses, human body language will remain a foreign language. Despite this they will show natural reactions to certain aspects of our body language. A horse may run away from us because it is scared when we give out threatening vibes, but this isn't because, as a dominance-based trainer would maintain, you are using your body language to teach certain exercises. Horses react to pressure by moving away and react to the removal of pressure by standing still. Horses trained using dominance-based methods will step backwards not because they have understood the lesson 'rein back' but because they are reacting to a perceived threat coming from their trainer. They will never perform individual lessons willingly but will react like puppets having their strings pulled.

The straightforward mechanisms of learning work in relationship to human body language as well. The horse will learn mostly negatively conditioned reactions, such as when the trainer reinforces their 'evil eye' by shaking the lead rope,

Horses that have been trained using methods involving pressure will often look scared when asked the easiest of questions.

running at the horse, or in the case of no reaction being shown at all, by hitting the horse with the rope. The horse learns that when one command is given it is followed by a further unpleasant action if it doesn't obey immediately. For this reason, in the future it will appear to react to the body language. But this is only because the horse has learnt to be afraid of the signals through their association with other punishments and training aids. This procedure has nothing to do with a person's empathy for their horse, but is a result of the way horses learn to behave. A horse would react to a robot placed in the middle of a round pen in the same way as it does to a trainer - even

Real horse play involves mutual understanding, role changes and a lot of fun. None of these characteristics will be seen during the so called 'play' contained within a system of dominance-based training.

if the robot couldn't imitate the aggressive body language shown by the trainer. As long as it was programmed to use the principles of pressure and release the same result would be achieved. In general, then, the question has to be asked whether it is desirable that a horse learns mainly from negative and threatening body language.

At play

Terms used in excess by many dominance trainers are the words 'play' and 'game'. These terms originate from scientific studies of equine behaviour, and as a result of their positive associations they are supposed to persuade you not to question the methods used. But do trainers really use play in conventional dominance training? It may be

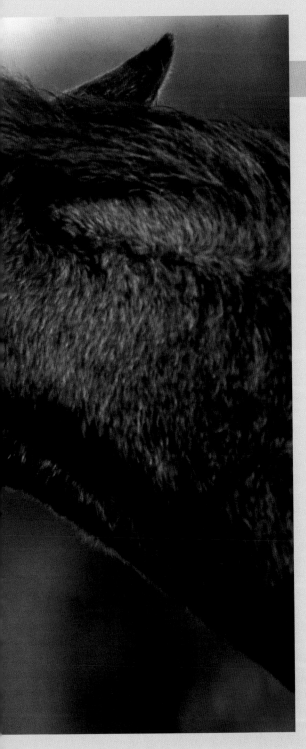

Foals make up games like 'pass the stick'.

true that some people see what is done as a game. However, true play behaviour, in a behavioural science sense, is not recognisable in these games. We don't see the usual sorts of playful faces pulled by horses at play, nor the gleam in their eyes or the types of movement they would normally show. Once again pressure is used to ask the horse to play, or rather to react. There is only one point in all of this – to demonstrate to the horse our superiority. Two equal participants are always needed to play, with the roles being swapped around and the activity being marked by fun and volition.

Under the guise of dominance training a new form of psychological pressure has become socially acceptable. It is pointless to consider whether psychological force is worse than physical, or whether how some trainers relate to their horses really represents progress – force is always force and should play no role when training a horse. Of course, not every dominance-based trainer acts threateningly, but the methods still create a negative atmosphere and remain a demotivating form of training.

Horse friendly

Enriching a horse's life

In recent years problems relating to dominance seem to have mushroomed. The explanation that the social hierarchy between human and horse has not been established is used to justify why horses show resistance and why they misbehave when ridden, as well as a variety of other signs of disobedience. As we have already seen, it is not possible to establish a true hierarchy using the methods of dominance training. Horses have to be educated and trained and every trainer has a choice as to whether they work with negative or positive methods during this process.

Many of the so-called problems with dominance are, however, homemade. They are due less to the relationship with the person, and much more to the often unsuitable management and care of the horse, to a lack of attention paid to the horse's natural needs, and to too many or too few demands being placed on the horse. In dominance training the real causes of the problems are frequently not addressed, but just the symptoms. A horse whose need for exercise is restricted owing to the way it is kept will always tend to fidget, rush and be generally stroppy. No exercises from the school of dominance training are going to help; improving the horse's living conditions is the only solution.

Essential for the soul: just letting a horse relax and be itself.

Let a horse be a horse

Modern and appropriate horse management should focus on the individual needs of each horse, as well as on the basic needs of the horse as a species. The more we deviate from this, the more frequently we are likely to encounter problems when handling or training our horses. Horses will look for outlets for their dissatisfaction and stress.

The most important prerequisites for a contented horse are the opportunity for exercise and movement, friendships with other horses, sufficient feed and water, light and fresh air. The horses themselves should be able to decide where they spend their time. The field or paddock must be appropriate for the number of horses and they should always have shelter available so that they can get out of the weather. It is true that horses love company but not every horse is suited to every group. The construction of a herd of horses living out together should be done with care, with the animals being watched carefully to ensure that the combination suits every horse's personality and its needs.

Horses are almost always hungry. It is not only a matter of consuming feed, but there is something integral to a horse's nature that requires it to chew. If the horse doesn't get enough roughage then it will look for a way to satisfy this need to chew.

Studies conducted over recent years have proven that horses don't necessarily move about more when they have a large area of turnout compared with a smaller area. If they have a bare, square-shaped paddock, the horses are likely to stand around a lot because there is nothing to stimulate or occupy them. The result is a bored group of horses, and as a result of boredom and stress the more aggressive of them will pester the others. Excessive aggression within a group is always a sign of stress, and is often not performed by especially dominant animals. Horses need some structure to their environment – they require plants, sources of feed, a trough to drink from, a sand hill or two, circular rather than square turnout and even branches to nibble on, all of which will give them something to occupy themselves with. Bare turnout that doesn't have grass should resemble a more natural grass turnout as much as possible. A field with plenty of grass is the best turnout of all, of course, if the condition of the horse allows.

One of the common causes of problem behaviour lies in a horse's inability to mix with others in a herd. Many horses, unfortunately, have never really lived within a herd. As foals they were kept with their mothers by themselves, later they may have been kept in a group of adolescents without the company of horses of different ages, and then later sentenced to isolation in a stable with only very short bursts of turnout. From day one horses

Keeping a horse under poor or inappropriate conditions will often lead to problems when handling, as well as to stable 'vices' and other behavioural issues.

need to be surrounded by other horses. Only a few days of isolation can lead to permanent psychological damage, which will often lead to difficulties when handling. Horses kept by themselves or horses that spend too much time in their stables will out of necessity see people as a vent for their

Putting a real mix of horses together in a group demands special care when introducing them to each other.

unsatisfied need for play and social contact. Stallions and geldings kept like this will tend to be naughty and very cheeky. They will rush ahead when being led and often like to nip or bite. This is not a problem relating to dominance – or the lack thereof – but usually just a result of the horse's unfulfilled need for contact with humans or other horses. It is not just hours spent training that will help to eliminate such difficult behaviour, but a combination of training and changes in the way the horse is kept that will lead to an improvement for both horse and owner.

You are unlikely to be successful if you expect to be able to turn a constantly agitated or disobedient horse into a well behaved one just by using dominance-based exercises. So long as nothing is changed in the way a horse lives or is kept, new difficulties are inevitable. Improving the horse's life is sometimes called a programme of enrichment. Every horse owner can introduce long lasting improvements in the way they keep their horses by taking advantage of turnout and referring to the many good books on more natural forms of horse management.

Horse-friendly training

Further reasons for a number of the behavioural and apparently dominance related problems are the demands – either too few or too many – placed on horses during their daily training routines. The work that a horse is asked to perform should always be appropriate to the animal's potential ability. Not every horse has to learn to perform a piaffe or to do a sliding stop. Some horses may constantly feel as though they are out of their depth in terms of the work they are being asked to do, and so may try evade the demands being placed on them by shying or spooking, being cheeky or trying diversionary tactics such as snapping at the lead rope.

Asking too little can also cause problems. In this case a horse will get bored and will tend to start being silly in order to get a reaction from us, in effect creating its own entertainment.

A system of horse-friendly training will be directed at the horse's physical and mental capabilities. As a rider and horse owner you should be in the best position to gauge from your own horse's behaviour and the way it expresses itself what is best for your horse. If my horse seems happy and relaxed, if it has a gleam in its eye, its ears are flicking back and forth and it has a playful expression on its face then it is likely to be enjoying our work together. If it shows resistance, shows little initiative in certain exercises and has a tense look on its face, then it is possible that the horse is being asked for too much. The way a horse appears can be used as an indicator of whether training is truly horse-friendly or not.

Horse and rider as a team

Only those who manage to build a relationship with their horses that is based on friendship and

A horse-friendly system of training should always be built around the physical and mental potential of the horse.

understanding can really benefit from this unique relationship. There are a variety of relationship exercises and tests that have nothing to do with the commonly used methods found in a dominance-based training system.

A simple question that gives a good indication of the relationship between you and your horse

Often you can see at first glance what the relationship between human and horse is like.

is to look at what happens when you meet. Does your horse allow itself to be caught from the field? A horse that has a good relationship with the people around it will acknowledge your arrival and, depending on its temperament and the situation, will look up, whicker or possibly walk towards you, all the while showing an interested expression on its face. It's not such a good sign if the horse runs away or doesn't react at all. Many owners of horses that are kept mainly in stables are often deceived about the actual state of their relationship because of the way that their horse greets them, apparently enthusiastically, when they enter the yard. In many cases the horses are pleased more about the fact that you are a sign that they are likely to be freed from their prison or fed, rather than being particularly thrilled to see you. Real conclusions can only be drawn about a relationship in situations where the horse makes its own decisions.

How does the horse react when it is spoken to by its owner? Many horses don't react at all to their name or to a friendly approach since they have simply never learnt to understand this form of communication. A sociable horse should react positively to human body language. Sociable and friendly horses prick their ears when they are spoken to, follow their people with their eyes and ears, and like being touched.

Do you know where your horse likes being scratched, what its favourite food is and which games it likes playing most? It is surprising how many people don't know how to give their horse a small pleasure and thus cement their relationship. It is so easy to go over your horse with your fingers and try to find out on which parts of its body it likes being touched and in what way. Some horses like being touched very gently, others like a really strong contact. Many horses love being scratched on the withers or the thigh, but few actually like being given the traditional pat on the neck.

When it comes to feed there are very clear preferences that are easy to discover if you take time to experiment with feed or treats. Of course most horses like carrots, but whether they prefer them to apples can really only be found out if you offer both of them at the same time.

When it comes to playing there are also significant differences between horses. Some like

A relaxed hack is a comfort for you and your horse and will strengthen the bond between you.

games involving lots of running about and will love racing you across the arena, while others are very mouthy and will enjoy picking things up with their mouth and carrying them around. Playing together will considerably strengthen your relationship with your horse.

It doesn't always have to be work: rider and horse enjoy time out together.

Creative time off

We all constantly run the danger of being taken over by the daily grind. It is true that many horses are creatures of habit who enjoy doing the things that they are used to. However, there should always be variation in the work you do together in order to prevent boredom setting in. It can sometimes be helpful to try more creative activities in some of your free time, activities that there is not necessarily an obvious point to. Amid the demands of competition, we all too often forget that for most of us riding is a leisure pursuit and that we are supposed to be having fun with our horses. It does you and your horse good sometimes to let yourselves go and just enjoy being together. Given that grazing is one of the fundamental occupations for a horse, simply sitting in your horse's field and watching them graze can help to strengthen your relationship. Your horse will see your presence as a positive sign and this will help to deepen their bond with you.

There are also a variety of toys that you and your horse can play with together. Ranging from large pieces of cloth and plastic tarpaulins to balloons and balls, anything is allowed as long as it can be enjoyed by both and there is no risk of injury. Circus tricks offer both human and horse the chance to develop and blossom, and will refine the communication between the two of you. Horses love to learn and increase their intelligence through play. It is important however that you don't turn these exercises into another training programme that has to be worked through and demands a certain level of achievement – it should all be about enjoying doing something together.

Many horses just like being out with their human and equine friends. Riding out leisurely with others or alone can be a good way of deepening and cementing friendships.

Learning by reward

In contrast to the learning techniques promoted through the system of dominance-based training, which are based on a principle of building up and then releasing pressure, positive training methods are based on rewarding the horse. Common to all of these reward-based methods is giving something positive and avoiding any negative influences or pressure.

Of course there will be times when a situation demands fast action and may require the use of pressure or force. We have to differentiate, though, between real dangers and conflicts and everyday training and learning situations. In the latter there is no danger to life and limb and the horse can learn in peace and quiet. Learning by reward has nothing to do with anti-authoritarian teaching or wrapping the horse up in cotton wool. It is a clear concept that any trainer can follow. Of course, it is the human who decides when and for what a reward should be given, and who therefore takes a leading role, in the positive sense of the word. A horse that has understood this principle will learn very quickly.

For us too it can be difficult to get rid of our own educational ballast. On the one hand we may have been brought up and educated in a system that has used negative reinforcement or punishment. We will all have experienced a variety of systems in our past that have used some form of pressure to educate us, from having to achieve certain grades at school to being grounded following supposedly unacceptable behaviour. Even if we haven't been influenced by the very modern concepts of hierarchy, dominance and leadership, then it is almost a 100 per cent probability that we have learned that riding and training involves forms of negative reinforcement.

But how does positive training work when we want to avoid putting any pressure on our horse? Positive training works by offering a sought-after reward when the horse does something correct and withholding this reward when it doesn't show the desired reaction. The horse can make its own decision and is not forced into action by its handler. Meaningful rewards satisfy one of a horse's basic needs. Feed rewards are particularly effective and easy to use. Other types of reward such as scratching, praise or games can also

Learning by reward isn't anti-authoritarian, but instead both partners have agreed on a mutual set of rules that can be used consistently. Horses learn particularly effectively when rewarded with feed.

be found in positive training systems. When using positive reinforcement the stage at which a reward is given is of crucial significance. A horse can only connect a reward with a displayed behaviour or action when the reward is given immediately the behaviour is shown, or at most a few seconds afterwards. Otherwise it won't know why it has been given a reward, which can lead to misunderstanding.

For any system of positive training it is important to watch for signs of the horse feeling content or settled. This includes breathing quietly, a relaxed expression on its face, the unmistakable sign of playfulness when the horse extends its top lip a bit like an elephant's trunk, a gleam in the eyes and actively taking part in what is happening around it.

Diagnosis:
A problem with
dominance?

When the horse
is misunderstood

Diagnosing dominance problems has become almost fashionable, but it ignores both the fact that scientists have cast grave doubts over the existence of this type of problem and that it is a diagnosis that can be made on only very rare occasions. Every sign of a horse lacking enthusiasm, showing reluctance, being uncontrollable or difficult will be stamped as a dominance problem, regardless of the more likely cause being based on pain, poor quality equipment, the way the horse is being kept or the way the horse has been raised. This is all because in putting the problem down to issues of dominance the person is placed in a controlling role. The question has to be asked whether the diagnosis stems more from the trainer's own philosophy and behaviour.

If you turn your back on dominance-based training you will discover a new level of friendship with your horse that strengthens the emotional bonds between you.

The dominant human as an environmental factor

Provided they have enjoyed a healthy up-bringing, horses are prepared by nature to develop relationships with other horses and adapt to their social structure. They are not prepared for a modern, dominant master who has decided that certain behaviour on the part of his horse should be seen as an attack on his own position of power, and therefore sees it as his purpose in life to treat any inappropriate or abnormal behaviour on the part of the horse, such as a wandering of the eye away from the exercise at hand, as a personal affront.

True leaders don't even ask the question of who is dominant and who isn't, because they are self-confident and don't take their horse's behaviour personally. They are more likely to consider how they can train their horse's behaviour more positively instead of constantly questioning their relationship. Those with a natural command over others are considerate and don't need to worry constantly that their horses are going to suddenly try to seize power. A 'dominant' person, however, will often turn their relationship with their horse into a constant battle – as if the horse has nothing better to do than to test them incessantly. Research has shown that horses aren't in a position to be able to test anyone. They are motivated by the moment, either because they have no other choice physically, or because they have not yet learned to act differently.

Many problem situations are caused by a human's forceful and dominant behaviour towards horses. Horses often feel subtly threatened by their people and appear, depending on their personality, to be unwilling, fearful, overexcited or apathetic. The ambiguous signals that are given out by people often unsettle horses and create their own problems.

If a person isn't, for example, totally convinced by the concept of dominance training, they won't be able to implement it properly, even with the help of instruction from professional trainers. We have to be happy in our own minds about what we are doing and be able to apply a method with a clear conscience. Many people feel a subconscious aversion to the concept of dominance because it doesn't reflect the emotional ties they have with their horse. A person like this will run into problems using a training method that is inherently wrong for them, while more positive methods of training may give them an easier and less problematic way of working with their horse.

Many difficult situations are worsened by confrontation. Loading a horse into a trailer often becomes a problem because it isn't done in an atmosphere of calm, but is instead left to the last minute before leaving for a competition. The stress felt by all involved in the situation escalates dramatically until it becomes a direct confrontation between two wills – that of the person and of the horse. Most riders appear to expect that every horse, even with no practice, is simply going to walk into the trailer. They see any misbehaviour as an attack on their own position and a deliberate disobedience by the animal. If loading into a trailer had been introduced from the start with patience, praise and a positive attitude it would probably never have developed into such a confrontation in the first place.

A person's adaptability and willingness to compromise are important when faced with difficult situations. A situation mired in problems needs to be analysed, not simply tackled without any thought. Only then can you relate the training steps to the actual cause of the undesirable behaviour, such as fear or pain, rather than just expecting a horse with problems to submit to your will. Compromise will often be necessary in order to get to where you want to go. This means that the real fear that many horses experience when walking into a trailer will only be overcome by a longer period of practice during which the horse learns to walk on to the trailer voluntarily rather than being forced by its handler to do so.

More important than solving problems is preventing them from occurring in the first place. Potential difficulties can be avoided well in advance through good horse management, a relaxed learning environment and positive training methods. Horses that like their work learn easily and have no reason to resist you.

Common problems and possible solutions

In this section I would like to give you an overview of the problem areas that are most often diagnosed as being due to issues of dominance, and then discuss what could be the actual causes. These causes are given only as a suggestion of the direction that should be explored further, because a complete solution would have to be worked out on the spot on a case by case basis.

be particularly aggressive, but on the contrary tend to be less often involved in fighting or other aggressive conflicts. A much more likely reason for the vicious cycle of aggression is pain, certain symptoms that tend to increase aggression such as those associated with hormonal changes or infectious diseases, as well as stress.

If these causes can't be found, then you may be faced with aggressive behaviour that has been learned as a defence mechanism. Whatever you do to tackle this aggression, your own safety should be paramount. Typical dominance-based training equates to training using confrontation but with added pressure. This can lead to a horse becoming more aggressive in response, which is why a positive approach is always preferable.

Disobedience

If a horse doesn't follow your commands but just seems to ignore them, this can also be put down to problems of dominance. The more probable reason, however, is that the horse either hasn't understood what it is being asked to do, that it physically can't do it, or that you are dealing with a animal that is an example of the passively stressed horse. Passive stress is shown by animals when they react to outside pressure with a complete refusal to work and very often with total passivity. In effect they withdraw into their shell. These types of horses can easily be driven into a state of learned helplessness by a rigid pressure-based system of training.

Aggressive behaviour

Horses are often diagnosed with dominance problems when they show aggression towards people or other horses, whether this is demonstrated by biting, kicking or rearing. Studies have shown that animals with a higher social standing tend not to

Dominance-based trainers frequently confront horses with stimuli to cause fear, virtually asking for disobedience.

Fear

Many dominance-based trainers claim that their methods can lead to an improvement in horses that tend to be anxious or scared of various things. However, this involves in effect 'forbidding' anxious or fearful behaviour using pressure, rather than working on the cause of the fear. Many trainers will get a horse to load into a trailer using a build-up of intense psychological pressure that forces them to comply despite their fear. In the long term, though, the horse will still be difficult to load because the owner or rider usually can't repeat the exercise by themselves and will still be confronted by the horse's fear. In a dominance-based training system fear is suppressed by learned help-lessness.

To work through fear you should never resort to methods that use pressure or the technique of flooding the horse with stimuli. Instead the horse should be desensitised gradually to situations that it is afraid of. A typical example of this is a horse that is scared of having fly spray applied. First of all the horse (not tied up) is shown the bottle and praised for looking at the object. The next step is to spray away from the horse to get it used to the noise and again praise it for standing still. Gradually the bottle can be sprayed closer and closer to the horse until the horse is actually sprayed itself, again all the while being rewarded. Only then can the horse get used to the situation in a more relaxed way and learn that the spray can is not dangerous but rather has something positive about it.

Some horses are by nature, owing to a traumatic experience or a lack of worldliness, more fearful in their behaviour. Getting a horse gradually used to something that can cause fear is described as systematic desensitisation, meaning that the horse is confronted with what causes it fear but only so far that it doesn't cause stress.

If this process of habituation isn't done step by step, but as fast as possible, it is described as 'flooding' the senses with stimuli. The horse is exposed constantly to an unknown stimulus until the fearful reaction decreases as a result of the exhaustion of its attention span, and the horse learns eventually that the stimulus holds no real danger. An example of this is 'sacking out'. A rider puts a saddle straight on a horse for the first time. The horse bucks and rears because of a strong fear reaction and, depending on its temperament, may show this form of defence mechanism for a long period. It notices eventually that it can't get rid of the saddle and resigns itself to its fate. It will never like the saddle, though, because from the start it wasn't a positive experience.

This type of confrontational training is very wearing and has many side-effects. In the case of very fearful or sensitive horses it can lead to real

An ethical and practical way to get a horse used to the saddle cloth and then later the saddle is to work in small steps and in a relaxed atmosphere.

phobias and pathological panic attacks or even to aggression. The horse can become a complete bundle of nerves that has no trust even in itself. Given that horses are always aware of their surroundings and will connect them with the stimulus that they are being confronted with, a horse will begin to connect you with the flood of stimuli and start to fear you, or in certain situations avoid you – a poor basis on which to build a partnership.

The worst risks are often not even mentioned, out of pure ignorance. When using this flooding method you must ensure that the horse cannot run away from the stimulus – in other words it has to be confined. In practice this means that most trainers, when trying a saddle on a horse for the first time, will use a high-fenced enclosure like a round pen that the horse can't usually get out of. This doesn't mean, however, that it won't try. Depending on their temperament, some horses will try to jump over or break through the fence, becoming an uncontrollable danger for anyone present as well as itself. A panicked horse becomes almost oblivious to pain and will incur severe injuries in order to get away from the stimulus, or the source of its fear.

Apart from the incalculable risks that characterise these methods, I find them morally reprehensible. No one should ever knowingly cause an animal to panic, especially when there are more intelligent and humane ways of training horses. Don't let anyone frighten or scare your horse just to get it used to a saddle or to get it on to a trailer. Horses can't stand up to confrontation or see the sense behind it, so we owe it to our horses to look after their psychological needs.

A more positive way of getting a horse used to the saddle would, for example, be to place the as yet unfamiliar saddle on a stand next to a young horse while they are eating. The horse learns that a saddle is an everyday object. Gradually you can introduce carrying the saddle around, letting the girth or stirrups make their usual noise and then start laying the saddle cloth over the horse. Only when the horse accepts the saddle cloth should the saddle be placed on its back, initially without doing the girth up. Gradually tighten the girth up and reward the horse for standing still. In the following

weeks and months the saddle can become a constant companion to the horse on walks or when being worked in hand, before moving on to actually riding.

In order to end up with a reliable leisure companion with whom you can enjoy long hacks, you will need to work on the horse's overall calmness and self-composure. A horse may well shy away from unknown objects or sounds, or even other animals. In short, the unfamiliar is scary. Given that when riding out you will encounter a multitude of unfamiliar objects, you should try to get your horse used to such things in familiar surroundings.

To improve the horse's relationship with objects that may cause it fear, such as umbrellas, plastic sheeting or rubbish bins, we need to carry out a programme of systematic desensitisation with conditioning against the objects. First of all the horse should gradually get accustomed to looking at the object in a relaxed environment (desensitisation), with the distance to the object gradually reduced. Unwanted behaviour such as fidgeting or nipping can be stopped by using rewards when the horse is standing quietly. This transformation of a situation that until that point had negative connotations with the use of positive associations is known in learning psychology as conditioning. The good thing about systematic desensitisation is that what was for the horse a negative situation ('I'm afraid of that big flapping monster') becomes, thanks to the reward given, a positive one ('Great, I recognise these flappy things, I get a treat when I see them so I am happy to get close to them'). With systematic

Aspects of horse welfare are often trampled underfoot in horse sport. Under the disguise of dominance the horse is portrayed as a potentially dangerous animal that can only be controlled by the use of psychological or physical force. A look into the eyes of horses trained like this often reveals the sad truth.

desensitisation you build up the exercise gradually so that the horse will always stay quiet and accepting of the situation. It is very important to ensure that the horse never gets the chance to respond in a way that you don't want, because this can worsen the situation and develop into a habit. For this reason the distance to the objects used for practice should always be great enough that you stay just beneath the threshold that would trigger a fear reaction. Outside of training, situations that could cause a negative reaction should be avoided at all costs, in order to avoid giving the horse any opportunity to develop undesirable behaviour.

You need to find out at what distance from a scary object your horse will remain calm. If your horse only just notices the umbrella when it is five metres away and starts to tense up when it is at three metres, then you shouldn't go below three metres when starting to practise. Gradually the horse will learn to accept the unknown, even without treats.

Friendship instead of domination

All of us would like to tap into our horse's emotions. We are looking to form a partnership that crosses species, a true friendship for life. This friendship is characterised by the fact that you are there for one another and that there is a feeling of mutual affection, or even a form of love, without demands or expectations. You aren't really a friend to someone if you measure your friend by their usefulness or perfect manners. There is no hierarchy in a true friendship, because both sides acknowledge and accept their strengths and weaknesses.

A friend for life

Horses are capable of maintaining friendships over many years. We too can enjoy this unique ability to form deep ties if we are prepared to open ourselves emotionally to our equine companions and allow this special partnership to flourish and grow. An essential condition for the development of such a friendship is to respect the horse's uniqueness and differences, together with all its special qualities. Only when we respect the horse and its very nature can we expect to earn a horse's respect in return.

To build an ethical and tenable system of working with our horses, more than anything else we require a trust that has been built on the basis of the predictability and clarity of our actions. Only when you are happy with what you are doing, and how you are doing it, will the horse really pick up your feelings for it and start to trust you. A horse will trust someone who radiates an inner strength and calmness as well as this genuineness of feeling.

You are the one who, in this unequal friendship, has to make the decisions on a day to day basis, because the horse isn't in a position to do so. You gain a huge and invaluable advantage, though, by assuming a quieter form of leadership in which the horse is persuaded of the necessity of doing certain things through positive experiences and the enjoyment of being with people. True leaders don't look at the horse as a subordinate in the relationship, but rather as a valuable partner.

Many of the well known exercises used in a dominance-based system of training, on the other hand, cause the horse to give up mentally and become psychologically resigned to its fate. It isn't obvious to any horse why it should, apparently for no reason, move one way or the other or allow itself to be touched all over by a stranger. Obedience exercises such as these will only really be carried out with any enthusiasm when they are being trained positively. This also doesn't mean that you shouldn't allow your horse to approach you in case he makes an assault on your position of dominance. Horses need this close physical contact when forming and cementing emotional bonds and friendships.

Generosity is the essence of friendship

(Oscar Wilde)

An invisible bond

Friendship forms an unseen bond between the personalities of humans and our horses. This relationship with our horses gives us a unique opportunity to be close to nature. Through this friendship an entirely new world is opened up, if we are prepared to behave with sensitivity towards the horse, appreciate its differences and if we try to see its world through its own eyes. Horses are well ahead of us in terms of their sensitivity and loyalty. Their expressive eyes are the windows to their souls. If you look into a horse's eyes you will learn much about its character as well as what it thinks of you. This mutual friendship allows us to develop a united 'we' while respecting and maintaining our and our horse's own sense of individuality, our respective 'I'. Both partners play an equal role and pursue the same goals.

Appendix

Further reading

Wendt, Marlitt:
How Horses Feel and Think.
Richmond, Cadmos Publishing, 2011

Budiansky, Stephen:
The Nature of Horses:
Their evolution, intelligence
and behaviour.
London, Weidenfeld & Nicholson, 1997

Schmelzer, Angelika:
Horse Behaviour Explained.
Glastonbury, Cadmos Books, 2003

Kiley-Worthington, Marthe:
The Behaviour of Horses
in Relation to Management
and Training.
London, J. A. Allen, 1987

Kiley-Worthington, Marthe:
Equine Education.
Stowmarket, Whittet Books, 2004

Lethbridge, Emma:
Knowing your Horse:
A guide to equine learning,
training and behaviour.
Chichester, Wiley-Blackwell, 2009

Mills, Daniel and Nankervis, Kathryn:
Equine Behaviour:
Principles and practice.
Oxford, Blackwell Publishing, 1999

Hilberger, Oliver:
Schooling Exercises in-hand.
Glastonbury, Cadmos Books, 2009

Simpson, Heather:
Teach Yourself Horse:
Natural horse management.
Grayshott, D. J. Murphy, 2004

Contacting the author
www.pferdsein.de

Marlitt Wendt's homepage has information on the theme of equine behaviour and creative training, collections of scientific publications referred to in this book, as well as dates for seminars and lectures.

Index

CADMOS

HORSE BOOKS

Klaus Ferdinand Hempfling
THE HORSE SEEKS ME

In this lavishly illustrated book, Klaus Ferdinand Hempfling explains his system of communicating naturally with the instincts and nature of horses. The reader follows the progress of Arab stallion Marouk, and Lusitano stallion Queijo, in discovering a confident and harmonious relationship with their rider. Giving comprehensive insight into Hempfling's methods, the horses' progress is documented step-by-step, uncovering old wounds in the process that have resulted in their difficult behaviour. Readers will discover the fascinating process of understanding horses through the fine art of body language.

344 pages
Hardcover, full colour
ISBN 978-3-86127-975-4

Erika Prockl
LEARNING TO RIDE AS AN ADULT 1

The usual daily stress of modern living means that adults, and very often even adolescents, adopt tensed-up and faulty postures, which have a particularly negative effect on the horse. Here is a modern riding manual with a completely new training concept specifically designed to counteract the problem: A perfect loosening-up programme, which relaxes and eases.

128 pages
Hardcover, full colour
ISBN 978-3-86127-908-2

Marlitt Wendt
HOW HORSES FEEL AND THINK

This is a fascinating journey into the emotional world seen from a horse's point of view. The information provided offers a good basis for horse owners to learn how to relate better to their horses, to develop a more harmonious relation-ship to their horses and to school their horses without using force but in a positive, pro-active way.

128 pages
Softcover, full colour
ISBN 978-0-85788-000-0

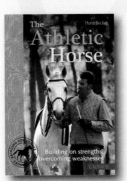

Horst Becker
THE ATHLETIC HORSE

When problems occur during a horse's dressage training, all too often the question 'Why?' is ignored. In this book, Horst Becker endeavours to find answers to this question. Whilst demonstrating ways in which a horse's weaknesses can be systematically corrected, he also shows quiet and effective ways of developing its strengths.

144 pages
Softcover, full colour
ISBN 978-3-86127-976-1

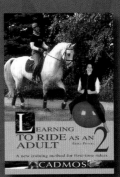

Erika Prockl
LEARNING TO RIDE AS AN ADULT 2

This second volume of Learning to Ride as an Adult is a modern manual of riding and movement instructions for riders with ambition, who want to ride their horses free of tension, with momentum, via the seat and with light aids. A special training programme is set out to help the rider to plan each schooling unit effectively.

128 pages
Hardcover, full colour
ISBN 978-3-86127-912-9

For more information, please visit
www.cadmos.co.uk

CADMOS

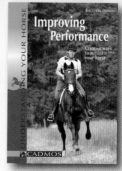
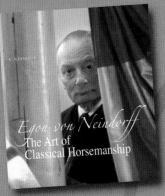